THE
CASH FLOW
INVESTOR

How to Create Financial Freedom
Investing in Commercial Real Estate

KEVIN BUPP

THE CASH FLOW INVESTOR

How to Create Financial Freedom Investing in Commercial Real Estate
By Kevin Bupp

© 2022 by Kevin Bupp

All rights reserved. No part of this publication may be reproduced or transmitted in any form or by any means, electronic or mechanical, including photography, recording, or any information storage and retrieval system, without permission in writing from the author.

Requests for permission to make copies of any part of the work should be mailed to the following address: kevin@kevinbupp.com

Published and distributed by Merack Publishing.

Library of Congress Control Number: 2022905690
Bupp, Kevin
The Cash Flow Investor

ISBN Paperback 978-1-957048-43-7
ISBN Casebound 978-1-957048-45-1
ISBN eBook 978-1-957048-44-4

DISCLAIMER

The information contained in this book is for information purposes only. The author, publisher, and distributor and make no representation or warranties about the content, accuracy, applicability or completeness of content enclosed. The information provided in this book is subjective and intended to provide helpful and informative material on the subject matter. Use the information in this book at your own risk. Your particular circumstances may not be suited to the examples illustrated in this book. All examples in this book are not intended to represent or guarantee that everyone will achieve the same results. The author has made every effort to ensure the accuracy of the information in this book was correct at time of publication. The book provides general information that is intended, but not guaranteed to be correct and up-to-date. Because the information enclosed is based on the author's personal experience and insights, it should not be considered as a substitute for professional legal, tax, financial, investment or accounting advice. All product names, logos, and brands are the property of their respective owners. All company, product, and service names used are for identification purposes only and does not imply endorsement.

DEDICATION

This book is dedicated to the three most important people in my life.

Joanna, my amazingly beautiful wife—who has supported

me each step of the way, and without whom none of

this would have been possible.

Jackson and Julian, my two incredible sons—you

are my inspiration each and every day.

I love you all more than words will ever express.

CONTENTS

SECTION IV | STARTING YOUR JOURNEY

FOREWORD

Wow! What an incredible resource for anyone wanting to learn this commercial real estate business. Kevin Bupp—by virtue of the world-class podcasts he hosts—has interviewed the best commercial real estate experts in the world on his *"Real Estate Investing for Cash Flow Podcast"*. He has used that wealth of knowledge gained from all the secrets and tips that come out of his interviews, and then of course his own success as a commercial real estate operator, to create this incredible resource. As a side note, Kevin is the reason I started my own podcast, *"Lifetime Cash flow Through Real Estate Investing"*. I was so inspired by his success in the space that I decided to try podcasting. I'm blessed and humbled to say my show has now been downloaded over 11 million times. All of that, and now the thousands of students that have been positively impacted, started because of Kevin.

In this book, Kevin lays out an extremely detailed step-by-step framework and blueprint for purchasing your first property regardless of the asset class. This is not some fluff piece like so many other "books". This incredible resource lays out the top five asset classes in commercial real estate, and then why they are the best. Kevin includes examples and case studies. This helps you to select the asset class that excites you so that you can go out in this lucrative commercial real estate business and create generational wealth for yourself and your family.

What I love most about Kevin Bupp that you should take special note of, is that throughout your life you typically only meet a handful of people that have "complete integrity". The ones that always live by doing what's right, regardless of the circumstances. I can honestly only think of about three people in my life that I feel that way about, and Kevin Bupp is one of them. That solid value-driven life, coupled with his love of helping others is what makes him so extraordinary. Kevin through his charitable efforts including his *"72 hours to Key West Bike Ride"* has raised hundreds of thousands of dollars for my foundation; "The Tiny Hands Foundation" and other worthwhile charities. The reason for Kevin's stratospheric success can be defined by this statement. "Power moves to those who serve" Kevin has a servant's heart and a deep desire to make the world a better place, and help anyone that he meets. That is evidenced in this incredible book.

This book comes with absolutely my highest recommendation, and if you haven't purchased it yet do it immediately! You will thank me. If you don't love it, or don't see the incredible value once you've read it, reach out to me and I will refund your money personally.

- ROD KHLEIF

Host of the *Lifetime Cash Flow Through Real Estate Investing Podcast*

PREFACE

Since day one, I've been an entrepreneur. It was this gut feeling I always had—the minute opportunity even seemed to present, my entrepreneurial mind kicked into overdrive and, suddenly, I was all-in and ready to not just dive in but take things to the next level.

At 12, I had a paper route.

At 14, I was selling car electronics out of my parents' garage.

I tended bar—and, quickly, learned how not to treat bartenders and servers.

I've owned more businesses than I can even name, from an 11-state event company to a custom sports apparel company, online education platform, mortgage company, and property management firm—among others. To me, every amazing idea deserves its moment in the sun—and I'm here to provide that moment.

But my biggest entrepreneurial venture? At 20, I dove head-first into real estate investing while attempting to finish college. I say "attempting" because I never quite made it to graduation day. Admittedly, after I saw the potential real estate investing presented, it was impossible to focus on anything else. So I left school and poured everything I had into my then-fledgling business.

If my kids asked, I'd tell them not to follow in my footsteps—to stay the course, finish college, and earn their degrees. But my kids aren't reading this so I'll say this: leaving school and dedicating myself to real estate investing was one of the best decisions I've ever made, and I'd make it again over and over.

For the last nearly-20 years, I've been all-in on real estate investing and consulting, delivering amazing results year after year. To date, I've completed more than $250 million in real estate transactions and that growth trajectory continues to increase.

But despite the net successes, things haven't always been so smooth. Through the ups, downs, and full-on knock-downs I've learned so much about real estate investing and entrepreneurship as a whole— things I wish someone had told me when I was young and ready to take on the world. While I might not have listened to everything—I was an idealistic 20-year-old, after all—having a clearly-defined and expertly-proven roadmap to success would have saved me from a lot of pain, disappointment, and missed opportunities.

Between the lessons learned on my journey up and out and the incredible mentors who stopped, saw my potential, and took me under their collective wing, I grew and evolved into the real estate investor and business owner I am today. And that's why, now, I pay it forward.

To me, that starts with my two top-rated podcasts, *Real Estate Investing for Cash Flow* and *The Mobile Home Park Investing Podcast*, where I dispense free advice to millions of listeners all over the world. Downloaded in over 190 countries, I share insights, intel, and information I've personally gathered from my years in the business-building trenches that I hope benefits other real estate investors coming up right now. If I can save them a little time, a few bucks, and a truckload of frustration, I've done my job.

That's why I'm writing this book. Again, for me it's all about paying it forward and giving back. It's about sharing what I've learned and continue to learn every single day. I see this as my way of consolidating and simplifying 19 years of lessons learned, missteps made, and decisions that, for better or for worse, led me here—to a life and career I absolutely love.

Real Estate Investing As A Vehicle

Real estate has created more millionaires and billionaires than any other type of business or industry in the world. The opportunities *are* there and waiting for you. I can promise you: this is the vehicle that can help you achieve whatever lifestyle goals you desire—and I'm living proof.

I've got a young family—two small children and a beautiful wife. Because of this business, I'm able to enjoy spending time with them and creating those special moments whether we're traveling across the country, out on our boat, or whatever it might be. Ultimately, real estate has allowed me the freedom and time to live a life I've always dreamed of.

I want that for you—and I believe real estate investing is the way to get there. No matter your background, age, interests, or what you want out of this life, real estate investing can take you there, if you have the right roadmap to success.

Over the last 20 years, I've invested in and owned so many different types of properties, from multifamily to retail to office, and everything in between. But today, my focus is cash flowing commercial real estate assets—primarily *mobile home parks*. Although mobile home parks have become my first love, the main concepts and strategies laid out in this book translate to all aspects of commercial real estate—no matter what asset class you choose.

How to Use This Book

Whether you've got previous real estate experience or just getting started, know that commercial investing is very accessible and much easier than most people think. With this book, my goal is to boil down the broad topic of commercial investing into easily digestible concepts.

Section One of this book covers the fundamentals of commercial real estate. I unpack and dispel some common myths about commercial investing (it's not as hard as you think!). I talk about why it's so important to uncover and act on your 'why' and why *that* should be your focal point in all that you do. Finally, the most important part: why I believe cash flow is king! It's all about the cash flow.

Section Two goes over the practical aspect of the business. This is what I'd call the "nuts and bolts" of making a deal happen. In this section, I'll go through the process of structuring a deal, from start to finish. I'll start with how I find and analyze deals, make offers, how I do my due diligence, inspections and more. I'll cover deal funding and management and much more. So section two focuses on how to pull all the pieces together and organize a deal from start to finish, to ensure success.

Section Three provides a special Bonus section encompassing *My Top 5 Most Profitable Asset Classes* to invest in. These include mobile home parks, multi-family, self-storage, assisted living facilities and parking lots. These segments are written by five amazing experts—experienced investors who have focused on and perfected investing in their individual niche. Once you understand the fundamentals of commercial real estate and how to do a deal, this bonus section will give you some insights on each asset class so you can determine which is right for you. This is something you don't want to miss.

Section Four talks about investing with a *purpose*, the importance of paying it forward and giving back to causes and people that we hold dear. This section also covers your 'next steps' and how to get started on your journey to commercial investing. We begin with strategic goal setting—setting up your big goals and breaking them down into mini, bite-sized pieces. Putting one foot in front of the other so you can achieve your goals and build your business. Section four rounds out by giving my final thoughts, and how we can work together in the future.

As you read through this book, you'll see quite a few commercial real estate investing terms. If you're unsure of their meaning, you'll find their definitions in the comprehensive Glossary in the back of the book.

While this book is very comprehensive, keep in mind—the commercial real estate investing industry is far too big to encompass *everything* in just this *one* book. So my hope is that you use this as a stepping stone into the world of commercial real estate and it helps you find your path to financial freedom through cash flow investing.

SECTION I
THE FUNDAMENTALS

CHAPTER 1

DISPELLING FOUR COMMERCIAL REAL ESTATE INVESTING MYTHS

I know commercial real estate investing can be intimidating—I won't pretend it's not. When I first started out, I was absolutely intimidated. Just the thought of investing millions and millions of dollars of my money or (gulp…) someone else's—was enough to send me scrambling right back to safe, simple residential investing.

Fast forward to today and, of course, I've overcome those hurdles and any other challenges that popped up along my journey. Now, I recognize the same fear and intimidation in others wanting to get into the commercial investing game. The worst part, though? In most cases, what's holding them back is all just a myth.

I'll say it again: what's holding back aspiring commercial real estate investors—possibly, you—from jumping in often isn't real. These hurdles are just myths we've convinced ourselves of, created or heard from someone else saying it can't be done.

Moving forward simply means dispelling any myths and instead believing, "*I can.*"

Let's look at the four most common myths about commercial real estate investing and then examine the actual truths so you can get out of your own way and start seeing real results in a big way.

Myth #1: You need a lot of money to invest in commercial real estate

This is one of the biggest myths and the excuse I hear over and over again. Commercial real estate is expensive, so clearly, a real estate investor needs a tremendous amount of cash and capital on hand to get started.

In a word? Wrong.

> **Truth: You don't need a lot of money to get started.**

You do not need a ton of money or backing to start investing in commercial real estate. While this is the hurdle people are most worried about, it's actually the easiest to overcome.

Granted, getting started *is* easier if you have cash in the bank, but going into a venture like this totally cash strapped can actually be a benefit. If you're cash poor but passion and commitment rich, you'll bootstrap, and *that* builds major character. In my experience, the commercial investors with personal capital aren't as resourceful and don't necessarily think through their decisions quite as much—and that's a problem.

On the other hand, the investors with little to no money to invest have *everything* to lose—credibility, trust and their investors' cash, for starters. This makes people very smart, very strategic and very resourceful from the get go. When everything is on the line, smart people hustle and *figure it out.* Those are the people who become incredibly successful as commercial real estate investors. More on the logistics of the money side to come later.

Myth #2: You need a track record of real estate investing success before getting started

Another common myth I hear is that to succeed—or even get started— in commercial real estate investing, you need a proven track record of success. Again, it's simply not true.

> **Truth: You don't need to have extensive experience to hit the ground running and make money as a commercial real estate investor.**

That said, there is *some* value to gaining experience in the residential market or with small commercial properties before swinging into large-scale commercial investing. But there's no need to spend years perfecting your process or buying into dozens of smaller investments before closing your first commercial deal. In fact, that's crazy, and will serve no other purpose but to keep you from achieving your long-term goals.

Get your feet wet—or don't—then GO. Tear down the barriers and smash through the hurdles holding you back. Understand the simplicity and clear-cut benefits to investing in commercial real estate, then *do it.*

Open your mind to the possibilities that are sitting right there in front of you—the shopping center, the medical building, the warehouse space—and start connecting the dots. Chances are you'll quickly see that commercial real estate investing isn't all that scary and doesn't require the kinds of lengthy, hands-on history you anticipated. That's empowering.

Myth #3: You will rack up tons of debt—and never get out from under it

Then there's debt. Debt is one of those things that strikes fear in even the most confident investor.

> **Truth: In commercial real estate, the debt structure is more complex than it seems, especially versus residential real estate.**

In residential, for example, the buyer or investor often takes out a simple, 30-year fixed rate loan from a bank or institutional lender. Alternatively, they may opt to work with a private lender, depending on their wants, needs, goals, and financial backstory. But, usually, it comes down to one of two debt scenarios.

In the single family residential sector, it's easy to set it and forget it when it comes to a property's mortgage. Your rate is fixed and that means you don't have to worry about it spiking every seven or 10 or 25 years.

You don't have to worry about getting new debt in place before your payments balloon. Again, set it and forget it—easy.

In commercial real estate investing, things are different. In this market, debt is definitely more complex and, often, shorter-term with amortization starting as low as 15 years. While you may be able to find an option in the 20- to 30-year range, most will be much shorter. As a real estate investor, you need to be prepared.

In addition, many of those shorter-term loans reset, usually around the five-year mark. At that point, your rate and your payments balloon unless you refinance. This involves taking out new, different debt or selling your investment property to pay back the loan—hopefully, with profit.

With that said, there's definitely risk to these debt structures. No one knows what five years will bring. I've seen rates increase three points in five years—not ideal if your loan is resetting. In that case, the shopping center you bought with a 5% rate is now 8%. It's drastic, but it's possible. As a commercial real estate investor, you need to be prepared.

It's a scary thought, though, even if you're a seasoned commercial investor. On a multi-million dollar loan, that rate spike could be severe and make that property a not-so-good investment, literally overnight. You might not even meet the minimum debt coverage ratio even though it was a non-issue when you applied for the loan.

I'm not sharing this to scare you, but to encourage thoughtful planning as you transition into commercial real estate investing. There's a complexity in this industry that investors need to continuously think about and work through. It's not about being comfortable, per se, but more about stepping into this realm, learning the complexities of the capital stack and, from there, learning how to underwrite the risk into your front end. This will steer your debt structure and what you opt to put into place. Done right, that will mitigate your risk and help you be a better, more lucrative commercial real estate investor.

With this in mind, the debt structure of commercial real estate investing—and lending in general—changes constantly. I'm always monitoring the capital markets to determine the best debt structure to put in place when closing deals. Just when I think I have it locked down, the market changes.

What's more—and what you'll soon discover—is that as your business expands and scales, you open up new options for debt and lending. As you get more assets in your portfolio and under your management structure, there's more opportunity to get in front of debt sources that didn't exist when you were a smaller fish in a much, much bigger pond. The bigger you scale, the more these otherwise unknown lending sources start to bubble to the surface. Sometimes they'll even pursue you—think about that for a minute.

Understand, there is—and always will be—some very inexpensive debt out there, especially on the commercial real estate investing side. To get your hands on it, you need to scale to a certain size and understand the complexities that come with this kind of lending. In the interim, there *are* options and, as you'll see in later chapters, plenty of them. You just need to know where to look.

Myth #4: The commercial investing industry is far too hard and complex to understand

Let's now dispel this common myth: that you can't get into this business because it's too hard and requires more foundational knowledge than you could ever hope to achieve. This is not the case.

Truth: You can perform well especially with a solid educational foundation in place.

Like the other myths, I do understand where this one stems from. In any industry there's a vernacular—lingo, industry-specific terms and other phrases that seem to differentiate the pros from everyone else. Commercial real estate investing is no exception. We have our own vernacular, and hearing us go back and forth can sound like a completely foreign language to someone who's new to real estate investing—to someone who's new to *commercial* investing, even.

Underwriting is also completely different which, likewise, tends to throw newcomers. If you're ever purchased real estate—even your own home—you've dealt with underwriting. In commercial real estate investing, it's very different. As a result, I think people write off the entire business. They assume they'll never "get it" because underwriting looks and feels unfamiliar. That's a big mistake.

In single-family real estate, investors purchase properties to fix and flip. It's all very simple from a valuation perspective. You calculate your after repair value with a quick formula, looking at repair costs and what you could pay for the property today. If it all aligns, it's a good deal—again, very simple.

When you're underwriting a $10 million shopping center with multiple holdings in place, multiple lease rentals and a handful of tenants, things get a little more complicated. Maybe the T-Mobile store is a great tenant with a clear-cut lease and market rate rent. But, right next door, you could have Bobby Jo's diner that's been there for decades, pays next to nothing and has a lease that feels never-ending. Each has a different risk profile with different credit worthiness. Already you can see why underwriting these investments is so much more complicated than underwriting a single-family fix and flip.

Overcome Your Skepticism: Gaining the Confidence to Step Up and Invest

Ultimately, if you're confident in yourself and your abilities, you won't worry about these would-be hurdles. You'll simply power through and build your business.

To get that confidence, though, you need one thing: an education. Again, this isn't about building a huge foundation (see myth #4 if you need a refresher). Instead, it's about knowing enough to be ALL IN—to want to move forward and to trust in your ability to get the job done. In short, yours should be an education in confidence—because once you have confidence, you'll feel good about moving forward in commercial real estate investing.

When I got started over two decades ago, there was virtually nothing out there when it came to commercial real estate investing education. No webinars, no podcasts, no investor club meetings. Anything my peers and I learned was done on the ground, on our own. It was a tough way to get started, but we powered through to build our businesses.

A lot has changed in the last 20 years. But what *hasn't* changed? To build your confidence in this industry, you need to get an investor education. You need to surround yourself with high-performing investors who know, do and invest more than you—successful people you can learn from just by being around them.

To that end, it's important to lock down a mentor or coach as soon as possible. These experts are invested in your success and, given their commitment and experience, can do wonders to raise your confidence and drive your investor education forward.

In some cases, you can find a willing and able mentor to take you under their wing—but, in my experience, that's rare. You may need to tap a paid option and hire a coach or mentor to train you as you go. That's perfectly fine. Strategically investing in yourself and your business is the single best investment you can make. And this book, hands down, falls under that umbrella.

If making a financial investment to find a coach or mentor is out of the question, consider the alternative: providing a value-add to that mentor or coach. If you can bring something unique and tangible to the table, that all-star mentor may be willing to help you build your business, in a big way. That value could be getting them involved in your deals and offering a substantial return for their coaching, networking and support. Or it could be providing some high-value service. For example, if you're a contractor, you could help them with their next fix and flip. Each potential mentor is different, so give some thought before offering up suggestions.

Ultimately, getting started with commercial real estate investing is just like anything else—you need to make a decision and commit, knowing there will be bumps in the road. But, at the end of the day, it's not rocket science. If it was, I wouldn't be here. It's simply a firm commitment paired with perseverance and persistence. That is *truly* all it takes to excel as a commercial real estate investor.

The Biggest Hurdle: Fear of the Unknown

That education-driven confidence has another very tangible benefit: overcoming the myths I mentioned earlier. To me, buying into these myths comes down to fear. Would-be investors worry they aren't ready for this or are terrified to fail. As a result, they make up excuses and allow themselves to fall into artificial roadblocks along the way. Each time they do, they push themselves further and further from their goal.

Fear of the unknown is a very big, very real thing. Having the confidence to step out of your comfort zone and into that unknown is a major step forward, no matter the outcome.

Interestingly, I have found that those who are the worst at stepping out of their comfort zone are the ones who are already mildly successful. They have a commercial investing system in place and they're making money from it. That's not enough; they want more. Maybe they've hit a wall or maybe they just recognize there's more out there. But, because they have that initial success to cling to, they refuse to take the steps necessary to find that "more." They may talk a big game or say they're ready for something new but, in the end, they aren't ready, and until they can shake their fear, they never will be.

Ever.

Whether you have cash, experience, *commercial* experience or the "right" education, you can—and will—succeed in this industry if you can get your cash flow in order. That's exactly what we're going to cover in this book.

CHAPTER 2
FINDING YOUR "WHY" & YOUR FOCUS

Steve Jobs is one of the most famous entrepreneurs in history. His iconic company Apple was the brainchild of a then 20-year-old Steve. With just $1,350 and some space in his parents' garage, he and his partner, Steve Wozniak, created what would later become one of the most game-changing companies ever. Apple has revolutionized everything from how we engage to how we work to how we live. It all started in that garage.

It also started with one small word that represents one big notion: WHY. I would argue that a "why" has powered every single innovation *ever*. We're curious, driven creatures by nature. Not only do we need to *know* "why," but we're constantly seeking to achieve *our* "why." The combination is a force like no other, capable of tearing down even the biggest barrier and transforming dreamers into doers and doers into thriving entrepreneurs.

The "why" is that powerful.

I suspect that there were many iterations of Steve's "why" over the years. Early on, he said he was driven by an unwavering desire to create a "computer for the rest of us." Later, he wanted to revolutionize consumer experiences, from how we listen to music to how we converse and engage. And, likely, underscoring every single moment in his storied career was some other "why" we'll likely never know—something deeply personal that kept pushing him forward, even when others predicted his and his company's demise.

Uncovering and Acting on Your "Why"

> "Desire is the key to motivation, but it's determination and commitment to an unrelenting pursuit of your goal—a commitment to excellence—that will enable you to attain the success you seek." —Mario Andretti

As commercial real estate investors and entrepreneurs, we are no exception. We, too, are driven by the power of "why." Your "why" is the impetus behind this next step—what's driving you to get started with commercial real estate investing. Your "why" reveals why you're investing, why you're starting a business and why you want to get involved in real estate in the first place.

By determining and embracing your "why," you'll be able to stay the course even when things get a little rocky. That's more important than it likely sounds. Committing to this industry means *committing*. This isn't some get rich quick scheme. Real estate investing is a dynamic career path that's helped countless entrepreneurs achieve their "why", and it's a surefire way to achieve your "why" no matter how personal and how lofty it may be.

So, then, the big question: how do you determine your true "why?" First, understand that everyone has a reason for doing anything and everything. Now, it's time to unearth why you want to get involved in commercial real estate investing on the deepest possible level.

Second, understand that your "why" *can't* be "money." Wealth and financial freedom are side effects of successful commercial real estate investing and, arguably, extremely compelling reasons to get started in this business. However, if your only motivator is a paycheck, then you aren't going to get very far. Why? Because when you have money, other voids will present themselves—money is just a temporary fix. Sure, you'll have the cash, but you won't necessarily feel or be fulfilled, and money can't help you there. Soon enough, you'll find other pain points, other reasons to hide under the covers and other challenges you likely never had or knew you had before money entered the picture. I've seen it happen over and over.

By finding your "why" outside of the dollars and cents arena, you'll be able to fill those voids now and in the future—a future where you *do* have lifelong wealth and financial freedom as a result of commercial real estate investing.

It's About People First

I have two young children and an amazing wife. That's my "why". My family is a relatively newer "why" for me. A decade ago, they weren't a reality, so they weren't a motivator. Now that I'm a dad, they are the ultimate "why" that keeps me pushing forward.

They're the reason I get out of bed in the morning and hustle all day, until my head hits the pillow.

They're the reason I'm always striving for bigger, better and more exciting things.

They're the reason I continuously take things to the next level *and kept pushing*—and will *always* keep pushing.

I want my family to have everything and more, and I'm able to deliver that through my passion, my conviction and my commitment. To me, that is beyond powerful. That is my "why."

Maybe that resonates with you. Maybe you're a parent and you know without question that your kids are your reason for doing, being and achieving. But maybe you don't have kids or a spouse, or maybe your life looks a little different right now. That's okay—great, even.

I would say to consider *people first* when determining your "why." The most successful people in the world always have someone standing with or behind them, helping them achieve their goals.

Facebook Founder Mark Zuckerberg had Steve Jobs.

Bob Dylan had Woody Guthrie —he even wrote his "Song to Woody" as an ode to his mentor and idol. Facebook COO and author Sheryl Sandberg was mentored by her college professor Larry Summers. Astronaut John Glenn attributes his success to his mentor and former high school Civics teacher, who showed him life could be even bigger.

I know I am who I am because I've had tremendous role models, mentors and coaches. I've had a myriad of people supporting my hopes, dreams and goals, even when they seemed completely crazy. These people helped my journey, both personally and professionally. They made me who I am today and made me want to give back and help others in *their* journeys.

That is, hands down, the "why" behind this book and the "why" behind my continued focus on coaching, speaking and mentoring. I suspect your "why" is anchored in a person or people—someone who has motivated you and made you strive for something better. Think about that as you're crafting your "why."

The Power of Focus

After determining your "why", the next step is focusing on your unique niche—a niche that syncs with the "why" you've established in the exercise.

By determining your niche—something that truly syncs with your personality—you'll be better positioned to craft a meaningful path from where you are now to your end goal. Because you'll be so in-step with this niche, you'll be more likely to stay the course until you're firing on all cylinders—until YOU'VE become a master of your processes and product and can achieve your "why" without missing a beat.

If you don't have this level of focus, you'll fail—period. I know it's harsh, but it's true. People who don't focus wind up wandering aimlessly, hoping to hit their end goal but never actually crossing the finish line. At the end of the day, these focus-less entrepreneurs and investors wind up back where they started, worse for the wear with nothing to show.

It's not ideal—and it's not you.

You'll have a "why," and from it, you'll have the kind of focus that drives a deliberate, determined path to success. You'll find your niche and put the proverbial blinders on—in a good way. Because once they're on, no shiny objects can distract you from your purpose.

Like your "why," your focus should be something that's uniquely yours—there's no "right" focus or "wrong" focus, just what appeals to and inspires you. A good focus is one that enables you to reach your goals. For example, you may hate the 9-5 grind and want to quit your full-time job to be an active commercial real estate investor. That could be such a compelling point of focus that nothing will stop you from achieving that goal.

On the other side, you may love your full-time job and simply be looking for supplemental income to fund an upcoming retirement or to have a passive income source when you do retire. You don't want to be an active investor now or ever. Commercial real estate investing is simply a cash flow source aimed at funding your future. That's great, too.

Maybe it's bigger. Maybe your focus is to build a true commercial real estate empire. You want to dive deep, replace your full-time income and then some and make commercial investing your new career. They're all very strong, very compelling and very valid points of focus, provided they are authentic and speak specifically to you.

The power of focus is about determining which path you're going to take right now. That path could, and likely will, change as your real estate investing business grows and evolves. Once you've mastered a specific area of this business, you'll no doubt want to diversify and try new things. But, at every phase, keep that singular point of focus to propel you forward.

Where many people fail in commercial real estate investing and, really, in anything, is that they get overwhelmed and start to focus on too many things. One goal has their focus today, and tomorrow, they're onto the next thing. While they may feel passionate and purpose-driven about each of them, they don't focus on any one thing long enough to really master what's needed to excel.

You know this person. Maybe you are this person. You're going to make passive retirement income as a real estate investor one day then, a minute later, a friend has a better, simpler opportunity to make big bucks. That shiny object—the new money-making potential—yanks you right off of an otherwise straightforward course, and you instantly lose any momentum you've built so far.

Every day is a "reset" where you're starting from base as if nothing has already happened. That's not a good thing. It is going to make your journey that much longer, that much harder and that much less purposeful—and if you can't shake this lack of focus, it's going to make achieving your goals virtually impossible.

When you focus, you're choosing something and sticking with it until you've mastered it. That's why you need to pick a core focus, put the blinders on and run with it until you get where you need to be. That's when you're free to pick a new focus and think about something else—something that's equally all-encompassing with strong momentum.

My mentor, Dave, was primarily a single-family home residential real estate investor with a few very small multi-family properties in his portfolio. His business model was strictly buy-and-hold for long-term cash flow. Everything he bought he kept and turned into rentals, building his lifestyle around that cash flow. While his focus and his immediate journey were very different from mine, he did teach me the power of focus.

He used to tell me that many of his friends were all about the fix-and-flip and they focused on those deals. They didn't like being landlords, they liked quick cash. That was their compelling focus. It's exciting to do a three-month flip and make $50,000. For many, that easily beats making $300 per month for the next 30 years. It's just a different strategy.

Back then, Dave used to say, "Kevin, regardless of your path, you need to focus." He would constantly remind me that there was not one path to success. Everyone—and every investor—is different and every approach is valid, provided it motivates.

I always liked and respected what Dave had built and what his core message was. His business model was incredibly sustainable and stable. I literally followed what he did and took what he instilled in me in terms of focus, gaining momentum as my business grew and evolved. I got good at one thing, then another and then another, attributing it all to the power of focus. I diversified, spread my wings and became a powerhouse commercial investor.

Today, I'm intentional about putting my head down and getting to that mastery level before pivoting and trying something new. Yes, my focus has strayed from time to time—as an entrepreneur, it happens. But I've always recognized it, course-corrected and didn't allow it to be detrimental to my business and my success.

Sometimes, though, I felt a bit alone in this approach. I would attend an investment club meeting and chat with my peers who had much more experience and, seemingly, much more success as real estate investors. One week they would tell me they were excited about buying homes with lease options, and the next week, they were going to start wholesaling properties. They were all over the place, with no focus and no commitment to their "passion." Everything was so fleeting and so temporary and, clearly, they never mastered any of it. I would see them a month later and they'd be onto the next thing.

Their excitement tended to follow the trends—what was new or hot in the market or what I saw bubbling up in the investor's club. While it's all well and good to take the market's temperature, listen to your peers and try new things, if you can't find your true focus and follow it to the finish line, then you're going to struggle in this—or any—business.

That's not what we want. We want to harness the power of our "why" and our focus to find our fortunes as commercial real estate investors. Then we want to rinse, repeat and do it all over again, this time with a new focus to chase and a new niche to master.

This notion requires even more attention and awareness during two stages of your career: the very beginning, and again once you've realized meaningful success. In the beginning, it's easy to slide back into old habits or, worse, into a pattern of being overwhelmed and falling off course. As you grow and scale—which is where I am—you'll find yourself pulled in a million different directions by peers and colleagues who present opportunity after opportunity.

In both scenarios—and at any point in your journey—you need to stay singularly focused and moving in the right direction: *forward.* Move toward understanding. Move toward mastery. Move toward your why. Only then will you be able to achieve your core focus and cross that finish line.

CHAPTER 3

MASTERING THE FUNDAMENTALS OF COMMERCIAL REAL ESTATE

While it may sound complex, especially if you're new to real estate, the approach in this book is surprisingly simple—so simple you'll be able to master the essential steps I'll be outlining so you can move forward like a pro.

Don't get overwhelmed, don't get ahead of yourself and don't think too much about what's next. Simply read on, take notes and start thinking about how you can apply these lessons to the real world—to your commercial real estate investing business.

Commercial vs. Residential: Understanding the Key Differences

Many investors come to commercial real estate investing directly from residential—either they've had success in residential and want more, or they've fallen short in their efforts to find and flip or fill single-family properties. Regardless, these investors are ready for something new—and commercial fits the bill.

To be a successful commercial real estate investor, it's important to note what I just said—"these investors are ready for something *new.*" Why is that phrase so important? Because, too often, people transition to commercial real estate investing assuming everything they know, everything they've done and everything that's made them a success in one investing class will make them a success in another.

The reality is a bit different. While, yes, having a basic understanding of the ins and outs of residential real estate will likely make you more comfortable and confident as you dive into commercial, the two aren't all that alike. I don't say that to scare you but, more, so you know it's fine to come to the table with no experience—and if you have some real estate know-how, that's great, too. Regardless of your background or lack thereof, it's essential to open your mind and be prepared to learn.

With that understanding, let's dive in and look at the key differences between residential and commercial real estate investing.

Evaluation

The differences between the two types of investing start from an evaluation perspective. In single-family residential investing, we use comparative sales analysis, looking at what the home is worth by comparing it to recently-sold properties in the area. If a similar property sold for $150,000, your property is likely worth about $150,000. If a similar property rents for $2,210 per month, assume yours will rent for about the same.

In commercial investing, we use an income approach. With this approach, investors evaluate the value of a property by looking at its "net operating income." This is calculated by adding up the total rent collected and dividing it by the capitalization rate, the rate of return on an investment property based on its expected income.

Brokers

Another major difference? Many commercial real estate investing deals happen "off-market," through brokers and agents. In other words, they're never listed on the Multiple Listing Service (MLS). The investors who close these deals are the ones with the right connections and the right brokers in their corner.

While in residential real estate you'll likely want and need a broker or agent, the majority of listings hit the MLS, and likely multiple listing sites. This makes the process much more democratized—anyone can purchase a great residential deal if they're willing to dig into the MLS daily. That's not the case with commercial real estate investing.

A good commercial broker has the right relationships and, with those relationships, can find you the right deals at the right time. Compare that to residential investing and the differences are clear. In residential, virtually every property is listed by an agent, and 95% of the deals happen as a result of these listings. The general public has access, anyone can make an offer and, again, the process is very democratized.

Appreciation

In residential real estate, even the best investors are at the mercy of the market when it comes to appreciation and future value. It's possible to have two identical properties in the same neighborhood with the same floor plan, same square footage and same granite countertops, and still rent for two different prices. You're always at the mercy of the market in residential and, often, the work you do and investments you make have very little bearing on how much income you consistently generate.

Commercial investing is different. When you invest in commercial real estate, you can easily force appreciation. Do that and you won't have to wait for the market to pick up—you'll be able to steer it in the direction you want and need when you want and need it. This allows you to control your own destiny.

Entities

Another key difference is the business entities involved. Each time you purchase a new commercial investment, it's important to start a new entity—specifically, a limited liability company (LLC). This makes your commercial investment a standalone business, with a holding company above all of the LLCs that manages the individual assets.

When you purchase a new residential investment, it often becomes part of your overall portfolio. If you created a brand new entity every single time you bought a single-family property, it would be cost- and time-prohibitive. So typically, residential investors put these properties in a land trust—which can make discovering ownership a challenge—or put several properties into a single LLC.

Cash Flow, Cash Flow, Cash Flow

Cash flow is king—that's one of the biggest universal truths between residential and commercial real estate investing. While you *can* build major passive income streams with both approaches, it's much easier to grow meaningful, sustainable wealth—and manage that wealth—if you focus on commercial real estate.

In terms of cash flow, that's exactly what we focus on when we source deals. We invest for cash flow to create legacy wealth. To avoid outsized risk, we only acquire true off-market deals that have positive cash flow in place from *day one* (more on off-market deals later).

Our philosophy is this: Real wealth is created and grows over time through buying right, and investing for the long term. So once we've purchased a great cash-flowing asset, our favorite hold period is *forever*. This strategy allows us to build a portfolio of assets which generates cash flow and builds legacy wealth for our families.

But first, focus on cash flow—cash flow is king.

CHAPTER 4
CASH FLOW IS KING

In the last chapter, I talked about my mentor Dave, who only had a handful of multi-family properties in his portfolio at the time—but he was great about generating cash flow. That was Dave's business model—the "Cash Flow is King" model, let's call it. Every single property he added to his portfolio was a buy and hold meant for long-term cash flow. In turn, that's what he taught me.

Years later, I'm well-established in real estate investing and have come a long way from single-family investing. But, what I learned from him still resonates—and still drives my business, even today.

When we worked together, Dave would bring me to networking events and introduce me to his friends and peers. Many focused on the buy and hold strategy like Dave, but others anchored their businesses in fixing and flipping properties. They didn't like the rental game. They didn't like being a landlord. They liked quick cash—making a

$50,000 profit in a single deal versus making $300 per month for decades to come.

I remember talking to Dave after an event, and asking him which path I should choose—should I take a page from his playbook and dive into single-family, long-term cash flow investments, or should I aim for one-off paydays like his friends?

His response still sticks with me to this day. "Kevin," he said, "there's no 'right' or 'wrong' way in this business. No one approach is better than the other. But there IS one way that's better for you, depending on your long-term goals." That gave me some serious pause and, sometimes, does today. At that point in my life and my real estate investing career, I liked and respected Dave's approach. To me, his business model felt doable and sustainable in the long-term, and that's what I wanted.

So that's what I did. Early on, I followed Dave's investing approach to the letter. Only then did I start diversifying and adding in more ways to drive income.

I still use Dave's same "model" to some extent—specifically, I still recognize cash flow is king and structure my investments accordingly.

Earlier, I said 85% of our deals are made direct-to-owner. This allows us to purchase off-market assets well-below market value—allowing for more profit and cash flow in the deal.

In this business—and in long-term passive income and wealth generation—cash flow is king. At the end of the day, literally nothing else matters—not appreciation, not going with your gut, *nothing*.

"Cash flow is king" should be your mantra as you work through this book and start pounding the pavement in the name of portfolio-building.

Where Appreciation Comes In

Commercial real estate is typically valued on income—the more income a property produces or the more you can make it produce, the more valuable it will be.

When most new real estate investors think about appreciation, they're thinking about **natural appreciation**, which is largely due to demand in the marketplace and long-term inflation. When a property naturally appreciates, it slowly increases in value over time.

In this case, the only possible appreciation you'll drive is through modest annual rent increases—assume around 1% to 5% per year per tenant. Granted, over time we'll have principal reductions—tenants paying down your debt or your note payment on it, for example. But the equity you create with natural appreciation will not be dramatic.

In these scenarios, it's more about building equity over the long-term than it is about shorter-term cash flow or driving added value through "forced" appreciation.

Forced appreciation happens when you increase the value of your real estate investment property by raising rents, adding amenities or integrating revenue-driving add-ons, for example—is incredibly important to us and is exactly why we buy distressed properties or properties with some meat on the bones. When we leverage forced appreciation, we can renovate the property and flip it or rent it out for more than it was previously worth. It's not uncommon to buy a property with rents 10% to 20% below market rate. We've even done deals where rents were 50% below market rate. A quick renovation and a simple rent increase will drop a tremendous amount of revenue to our bottom line, ultimately raising the value of that property.

Let's take an example. Say you bought a mobile home park 12 months ago—nice mobile homes that look like single-family homes and cost about $50,000 each. They're well maintained on spectacular grounds, with lots of mature residents already living there.

While you got a good deal, this investment was far from a steal and, now, you need to force appreciation. Prior to acquisition, you noted a few minor capital improvements which need to be made—fixing roads, trimming trees, and improving landscaping. Everything else is in good or even great shape. So, you go to work in the first year improving the property after acquisition, making it a nicer place for the residents, and ultimately enriching the lives of everyone in the community.

Now, you've owned the property for a year and it's time to force appreciation by raising the rents. Let's say you've been renting each of the 125 homes in this park for $260 per month. By simply sending a letter notifying residents—and adjusting marketing outreach and upcoming rent agreements—you can increase rents and drive more monthly cash flow. You've spent *nothing* except the time to write the letters and the cost for the envelopes, paper and stamps—essentially, *zero.*

But, the impact is huge—this is the power of forced appreciation in action. Just think about it—if you decided to increase rents by $80 per month, you could generate significantly more monthly and annual revenue.

ORIGINAL INCOME	$260/month x 125 units = **$32,500/month** $32,500 x 12 months = **$390,000/year**
INCOME AFTER FORCED APPRECIATION (*Increase rents by $80/month = $340/month*)	$340/month x 125 units = **$42,500/month** $42,500 x 12 months = **$510,000/year**
OVERALL REVENUE INCREASE	**+$10,000 per month** **+$120,000 per year**

In this scenario, we've instantly forced the appreciation and increased our monthly cash flow by $10,000, or $120,000 annually. The best part is that we've generated this additional cash flow and increased the value of this investment without spending any more on management, maintenance or marketing.

Another way to force appreciation is to find and invest in a property that's being run inefficiently. Maybe the operating expenses are too high, maybe there are too many stakeholders involved in every decision, maybe they have too many people on payroll or are paying a useless management company to drive their property into the ground. Either way, though, the current owners don't have a good handle on expenses, workflows and tenant needs, and that's negatively impacting net operating income (NOI).

In these scenarios, as the new owner and steward of capital, our job is to increase the NOI as soon as possible. By doing this, we're directly increasing the value of the property.

Cash Flow is Still King

While appreciation matters, cash flow is still king. Even with solid appreciation potential, a deal has to be self-sustaining—it needs to support itself, at the very least, paying its debts, paying the investors and giving them a solid return from day one. This can only happen if the right cash flow exists. Because, at the end of the day, cash flow is king in this business—it always has been and it always will be.

SECTION II
THE PROCESS

CHAPTER 5
SELECTING YOUR IDEAL INVESTMENT VEHICLE

While residential real estate tends to be more homogenous—single-family homes or multi-family homes—commercial real estate spans countless asset classes, as well as various sizes, scopes and cash flow potential. By understanding the market, the asset classes available to you and how each can support your goals as an entrepreneur and a commercial real estate investor, you can begin putting the pieces together and identify the right investment vehicle.

Understanding Your Investment Goals

It's important to understand your specific real estate investing goals and parameters. No two real estate investors are the same and, likewise, no two investors have identical investing goals. A good deal for you could be a terrible deal for another investor, and vice versa. And that means you can't just go in and buy blindly in the name of positive cash flow. You need to understand what you invest in and why you invest in it and, from there, create your own personal rules of the real estate investing road.

Ultimately, it comes down to two questions:

1. What do you want to own?
2. Where do you want to own it?

The first question refers to the "**asset type**." Asset types can include:

- Multi-family properties
- Senior living communities
- Mobile home parks
- Office buildings
- Retail properties
- Strip centers
- Power centers
- Self-storage facilities
- Industrial parks
- Flex spaces
- Land
- Parking lots

That's just the beginning. Any specific type of property can be grouped into an asset class. Within each asset class there tends to be other specifications. For example, you could focus on multi-family properties that are specifically for low-income or Section 8 tenants. That's a unique niche that could apply to your chosen asset class and, as a result, would impact how, when and where you invest.

Beyond that, think about geography—where *specifically* you're investing. This doesn't just mean the immediate geographic location, though that plays a role. Geography can encompass the immediate area surrounding a commercial investment. For example, is the neighborhood desirable and poised for growth, or is it considered the "bad" part of town? One market—one neighborhood, even—could have multiple geographic "classes." And, unlike residential real estate investing, the "best" classifications may not always be the most desirable.

Five Core Asset Types

While there are countless asset types, for our commercial investing purposes we're going to focus on a few core classes. These asset classes tend to be the most lucrative and the most manageable, especially for first-time commercial investors.

Keep in mind, there are classes and specifications within each asset class—depending on your market, your budget and the immediate demands in your chosen geographic area, there could be specific niches that make sense for you to consider. For example, in a college town, a multi-family building targeting student renters could be the way to go. In that immediate market, though, you may see less of a demand for senior housing, at least near the college campus.

Let's take a closer look at the five core asset types.

Asset Type 1: Office Buildings

Office buildings can be a solid asset class in the right market. With lengthier leases—assume 3-5 years—and professional tenants, there's little to worry about once an office space is filled.

Cash flow tied to office building investments tends to be extremely market-dependent—if the economy dips and unemployment increases, office leases can wind up being reduced (i.e. a tenant shifts from renting three floors to renting one) or not renewed at the end of the lease terms. That said, with the boom in home offices, flexible work arrangements and co-working spaces, the economy may not be the only challenge to keeping these spaces filled with paying tenants.

And when you *do* have solid professional tenants? It's essential to keep tabs on ROI. Office buildings tend to come with higher broker commissions and sometimes-hefty tenant improvement allowances. Be sure to account for these costs in your upfront analysis or you could be losing a major chunk of your profit.

PROS:

- Longer-term leases (usually 3-5 years, minimum)
- Professional tenants
- Strong economy drives greater demand and higher rents
- Relatively low management challenges

CONS:

- Lengthy vacancy periods
- Heavy competition, including office buildings, flex spaces and work from home (lack of need for office space)

- Tenant improvement allowances and renegotiations
- Unemployment reduces demand—tied to the immediate economy
- High broker commissions
- Rental appreciation is cyclical

Asset Type 2: Retail

Depending on the market and the tenant, retail may also be a good go-to for commercial investors. Here, you'll wind up with net lease structures and triple net leases—in other words, you can bill the tenant for triple net charges while passing through common area, maintenance, real estate taxes and other operating expenses. All of this comes back to the lessee as additional rent.

The challenge, though? Most retailers want to customize and build out their space—and these unique spaces can be tough to fill if and when they leave or go dark. However, if you're able to lock in a major retailer or chain outpost, you could be looking at a 20- to 25-year lease—so any fears about leasing post-build out won't need to be dealt with for decades, *literally.*

When you do lose a tenant, retail spaces tend to be well-positioned—in high traffic locations, or near other shops and amenities. Keep an eye for locations that aren't overbuilt but that have potential for businesses beyond your current tenant. Retail has a tendency to drive long-term vacancies—finding a good spot will help you avoid that hurdle.

PROS:

- Economy drives demand
- Tenant build-outs are negotiable
- Multi-year leases with net lease structures

THE CASH FLOW INVESTOR

- Easy management

CONS:

- Tend to be oversaturated/overbuilt
- Tenant build-outs can be tough to repurpose
- Prolonged vacancy—often "go dark"
- Rental appreciation is cyclical

Asset Type 3: Industrial

Industrial properties tend to be very easy to manage. More importantly, there are lots of different niches under the "industrial" umbrella so, for many commercial investors, it's easy to find opportunities within this asset class.

Because of the nature of the businesses that seek out industrial space, owners and workers tend to be very hands-on and can problem solve as issues arise—this, often, keeps maintenance and other challenges off of your plate. This plus net lease structures can make industrial a go-to asset class.

There can be challenges, from environmental hazards to long-term vacancies. In terms of environmental issues, be sure you do your due diligence upfront—once you've invested, dealing with major contamination, pollution or other issues can be challenging if not completely deal-breaking.

As for vacancies, be sure you're coming into an area that isn't oversaturated. It's not uncommon for an industrial tenant to leave the area and completely decimate the landscape and the economy—it's tough to find another major tenant and employer to replace some of these major manufacturers or producers. However, if there's some versatility to your space or it can be divided or unified easily, you may be better positioned to keep the tenant rolls filled and the cash flow coming.

PROS:

- GDP drives demand
- Tenant build-outs are negotiable
- Multi-year leases with net lease structures
- Easy management

CONS:

- Potential environmental hazards
- Low barrier to entry in most markets
- Prolonged vacancies
- Prone to functional obsolescence
- Rental appreciation is cyclical

Asset Type 4: Land

Managing land is *very* easy—there's virtually nothing to take care of with these investment properties. Beyond that, though, these investments are net lease structures, enabling you to lease the land out—another bonus.

As market conditions improve, land can be a great investment—more businesses, retailers and companies will likely be interested in leasing your land, or you can opt to develop and lease out yourself.

There are some challenges. Even when land isn't actively being used, owners still need to pay property tax and insurance. This can eat into your future profit potential if the land sits for too long, so be sure you're investing with a clear-cut strategy for monetizing your investment over time.

PROS:

- Net leased structures
- Develops with market expansion
- Easy management

CONS:

- Environmental liabilities
- Real estate taxes and insurance even when there's no cash flow
- Can be slow to appreciate
- Value impacted by building demand and cost to build

Asset Type 5: Multi-family Properties

No matter your market or the state of *the* market in general, people always need a place to live—and if you can supply affordable, high quality housing, you'll be in business.

Many commercial investors favor multi-family properties because they're easy to understand and rarely have long vacancy periods. What's more, these properties are almost always quick to respond to market rents—unlike long-term leases, these leases tend to increase over time, driving more revenue to your bottom line without any added resources or commitments. Every month or two, as existing tenants leave and new ones come in, you're able to adjust your rent rate. Though seemingly minor, these increases can add up over time, especially in larger buildings.

People just "get" multi-family properties—everyone has engaged with residential real estate at some point, whether they rented or bought a property to live in. This perspective can help you make better investing decisions and better structure these deals—or, at the very least, make decisions with your tenants' best interests in mind. Because these are people's homes, expect those middle-of-the-night calls—and expect to be very engaged with maintenance and repairs.

PROS:

- Affordable, high quality apartments and condos are always in demand
- Quick to adjust to market rates
- Limited vacancy periods
- Economy of scale
- Easy to understand
- Competitive

CONS:

- Lead paint and other health hazards
- Tenant trends—can be negative
- Gross lease structures
- High repair and maintenance costs
- Very hands-on management

Riches are Made in the Niches

These are just some of the asset classes you can focus on. There are others, and there are niches within these classes. So, for example, your multi-family property could be college housing or affordable senior housing or Section 8 housing. Or you could opt for office buildings with a focus on small businesses—single office rentals, shared workspaces and as-needed amenities like conference rooms and teleconferencing spaces.

Ultimately, your asset class and specific niche are up to you and should be dictated by both your market and the current economic climate. There *is* something compelling about choosing a true niche—not just multi-family or land or office space, but really getting into a very specific and ideally very lucrative niche that you can dominate. In this business, riches are made in the niches—if you can find and dig into that niche, you'll quickly become THE expert. Hands down, the expert gets the business over and over again.

The Power of Mobile Home Parks

While you should choose the asset class and niche that's right for you, your business, your goals and your current market conditions, there is one asset class niche that tends to pop to the top regardless: mobile home parks.

Mobile home parks are an incredible commercial investment opportunity. I've personally invested in more than $100,000,000 in mobile home parks, and continue to spend a significant proportion of my time, talent and resources on this asset niche.

In my opinion, mobile home parks are the best type of commercial real estate you can invest in. Why?

- They deliver the best returns
- There's limited supply—but limited competition
- There's limited barrier to entry
- They're always in demand

No matter the market, mobile homes are always in demand. And if you have them, *you'll* always be in demand.

There's also less institutional competition in the niche, which is another plus. Even though there's limited supply when it comes to mobile home parks, there are also fewer players in the market. Everyone invests in single-family homes. Everyone invests in apartment buildings. But because so few people understand the unparalleled value of mobile home parks, these investments have historically flown under the radar. With limited supply, ever-increasing demand, and limited competition, mobile home parks create the perfect storm for any commercial real estate investor.

And that perfect storm continues whether it's a strong economy or not. Even in the worst times, people need housing and, often, mobile homes present that opportunity to have a quality place to live within limited financial means. In many cases, renters can move into an amazing, high quality mobile home for less than a sub-par apartment in a less than ideal neighborhood. While some mobile homes rent for different rates, the average in my portfolio is around $300 to $350 per month. There's virtually nowhere you can rent an apartment for that price.

Given this affordability, mobile home parks tend to have the lowest default rate of any commercial asset type. When the market is good, there's still a need for affordable housing. And, again, when it dips, there's an even greater need. For investors, it's a win/win.

CHAPTER 6

FINDING THE RIGHT PROPERTY

Successful commercial real estate investing is not just about getting a deal, it's about finding the right properties in the right asset class in the right market.

To do that, you need to be prepared to look beyond price and dig into the economic drivers, market conditions and population demand that make a market—and, with it a property—desirable.

Keep in mind, that doesn't mean only looking at the best markets or the nicest properties. In many cases, it means the opposite. If there's demand and your property syncs with the conditions and the surrounding population, you're likely in good shape—and you're likely on the brink of creating meaningful, long-term cash flow from your commercial investments.

The Importance of Market Selection

Too often, new commercial investors price shop. They have a number in mind and they pound the pavement, looking for a deal that they believe makes sense—a deal anchored solely in a price point. That's a problem.

I was presented with several mobile home park "opportunities" from brokers during the North Dakota Bakken shale oil boom. And the numbers looked good—almost too good. If I would have been buying on price point alone, I would have taken these deals down. And I would have eventually gotten crushed.

North Dakota had experienced rapid economic expansion due to the oil boom. With advancements in fracking technology, landowners were able to tap into large oil reserves that were never before reachable. It was a modern day gold rush, and oil workers from around the country flocked to get in on the action. Each of them needed housing. So many mobile home parks—basically man camps—sprung up to create supply for the housing demand. But when oil prices dipped, these mobile home parks became ghost towns. All that income—which looked so good on the brokers' proforma—was gone. The market economics didn't justify making an investment.

Market select is critical to success as a commercial real estate investor. Again, buy on price point and you'll wind up with trophy assets that never realize their full potential—they're in markets no one wants to live in, work in or shop in. The reality is, it's always better to have an "ugly" property in a dynamic market than the greatest property ever in a completely dead end market. If a property is incredible but generating zero income, it's worthless. That's the opposite of what you want as an investor.

Population Growth

It's supply and demand—Economics 101. If more people are moving to a market, there will be greater demand for the apartments, shops, office spaces and parking lots in those markets. Likewise, if a population is declining—if people are leaving an area—there will be fewer tenants, fewer shoppers, fewer business owners and fewer people filling your spaces. In other words, creating consistent cash flow will, likely, be a struggle.

Employment Diversity

Invest in a manufacturing town that produces a very specific type of auto part and, chances are, you're rolling the dice. If this auto part become obsolete—or if production moves out of the area or even out of the country—your investment could take a nosedive, even if the space didn't directly relate to manufacturing.

Think about it—that production stops and people lose their jobs, which almost immediately impacts residential rentals. With less disposable income, residents shop less, which impacts retail spaces. Eventually, without a replacement business, populations start to decline as people leave to find new work.

If a market has strong employment diversity, you'll have little to worry about. But in a one-horse town, there's always the risk that the sole source of income and employment could dry up—and dry up your investment with it.

Look for an area that has the underlying fundamentals to support diverse employment and economic growth—hospitals, schools, retail and other signs of life.

Pro-business Government

Be sure to check out the local government scene and see what they're doing to stimulate economic growth—especially for small businesses. Many areas, for example, incentivize companies and entrepreneurs to do business in their markets, offering tax incentives, local grants to help growth and other cost-cutting benefits to setting up shop in the community.

Local governments should be focused on getting new business and new residents to its borders. The most pro-business governments will be overt in their efforts to do just that, whether it's prompting residents to "shop small" or offering incentives plus, simply, making it easy to set up shop in their communities. Smart governments know their residents need places to eat, shop and do business, and they're making it a priority to ensure that happens.

Economic Drivers

Economic drivers tend to be a good indicator of what's happening and what's emerging in a particular market—and that can be indicative of your ability to find quality tenants or flip a commercial property.

Median income is a good basic gauge of a market—specifically, how well the residents are doing professionally and financially. While you don't want to base 100% of your decisions on median income, this quick-hit indicator does give a sense if a community is struggling, thriving or falling somewhere in between. A market with a $22,000 median income is very different than one with a $190,000 median income—and, with that, so are the rental, commerce and business opportunities.

Looking at median income isn't simply about a "have" or "have not" mentality. A low-income market can still present opportunity if your investment properties are in-line. For example, if you're renting apartments for $1,500 in an area where the median income is $22,000 per year, you won't have much luck filling them. However, if you have a high end mobile home park with homes renting for $300, you'll be better positioned to fill your properties and generate consistent cash flow.

It's also important to consider the job market. First, look at companies in the immediate area—are they coming, going or staying put? That, often, is in-sync with job growth or declines—if companies leave the market, often the jobs go with them. If you're investing in commercial space, that's important to know so you can anticipate whether you're renting apartments, warehouses or office space.

Schools

Regardless of a person's own educational background, household income, position—regardless of *anything*—people want good schools for their children. When you're considering apartment buildings or should you find yourself veering into residential, look for properties in good school districts. They don't have to be number one in the rankings, but they do have to be solid, well-performing schools that are safe and sought-after. If you have that, you'll always have a market for buildings.

We've bought properties in less than desirable areas—areas that are rough, rundown and, as a result, completely overlooked by other commercial real estate investors. However, these properties happened to be zoned for incredible schools—it happens. And we knew going in that, even though the properties were rough, plenty of parents would be interested in those apartments because, simply, they want the very best education for their children. If they can get into these A+ school districts, they'll do just about anything—including pick up and move into these buildings.

We knew if we could fix up these properties, we'd be in an even better position—we could attract even better, higher paying tenants who *also* wanted access to these schools. No matter what we did—or didn't do—these investments are always wins. If you've got the schools, tenants will follow.

Being in a solid school district makes sense even if you aren't investing in apartment buildings. If a person works in a community, they often want to live nearby. If your retail space, office building or warehouse is zoned for top-tier schools, chances are you'll attract local tenants looking to spend money in their immediate market—*if you work there you'll want to live there, and if you live there you'll spend your money there.*

Asset Classification Grades

Location is also important in understanding asset classes. Each asset class has different classification grades.

Mobile Home Parks are graded on a scale from 1-5 stars. This is partially based on location—in this case, it's the immediate park that surrounds and both the quality and amenities associated.

A three- or four-star community, for example, is a nicer, well-positioned mobile home park that caters to an affordable crowd. Often, these parks are mixes of older and newer homes, with a clubhouse facility, larger lots and a better proximity to outside amenities, interstates and secondary roads.

Keep in mind, it's easy enough to turn a lower-star mobile home park into a four- or five-star one. Recently we picked up a depressed mobile home park in a very poor area in Georgia—it had been hit very hard in the 2008 recession. The park isn't far from a private university so, even though we weren't keen on the investment, we knew that school wasn't going anywhere—having an anchor business like that means there will always be *something* keeping the community afloat.

Even so, we weren't sold on the investment. We went ahead and made an incredibly low offer—$100,000—on the foreclosure property and, to our surprise, it was accepted. Ten years earlier the park had sold for $1.6 million. And, now, we're in the process of getting it from a 1.5 star to a 3.5 star—or higher, even—and restoring its former value. It's doable and, while you're in the process of rehabbing and renovating, you can also keep generating consistent revenue. That's a win/win.

Multi-family Properties are graded on an A through D scale, with "A" being the nicest and "D" being a rougher neighborhood. In some "D" neighborhoods, you might not want to be out alone at night—some are that bad.

Office Buildings use an A through C scale, and the spaces range from swank to dank. Class "A" buildings are coveted, luxurious, highly-sought spaces, usually in a central business district. Class "C" structures are older buildings located in less desirable areas. They usually have deferred maintenance, out-of-date furnishings, and lack modern amenities.

Industrial Buildings are graded on an A through C scale, with "A" being top tier and "C" being the least desirable. Class "A" construction is usually impeccable with high-quality infrastructure. Class "C" buildings command the lowest rental rates. They often have unpermitted structures or electrical, and it can take some serious capital expenditures to get them back in shape.

No matter what asset class or grade you buy into, these strategies and considerations apply. And, as we did with the mobile home park, it's possible to upgrade your asset's rating with some simple work and resource allocation. While you likely can't change the neighborhood, you can change factors in and impacting your property—and, ideally, support the growth and evolution that leads to higher classification ratings and increased property values.

On Market vs. Off-Market Transactions

In commercial investing, on-market commercial real estate is exactly how it sounds—commercial investment properties that are listed on the multiple listing service (MLS), with a broker, or commercial real estate listing sites. Most times, these assets are sold at market rate.

However, the majority of properties never "officially" hit the market—they are "off-market" deals and you'll never see them listed on the open market or any listing site like Zillow or the MLS or Loopnet. These assets are sold sold below market value.

Is it actually better than buying an investment property that is listed through a brokerage company? Well, it depends on the true definition of "off-market".

Four Types of Off-Market Deals

There are four different types of off-market commercial deals available in the marketplace. While there are four types of off-market commercial deals, the only true off-market deals are direct-to-owner transactions.

Deal Type #1: Direct-to-Owner

This is what I would consider the definition of a *true* off-market deal. In this situation, the buyer is working directly with the owner to acquire the property. There's no broker involved, which is great for the seller because they won't have to pay a broker commission fee, and it's a huge plus for the buyer because it allows them to negotiate in a non-competitive, off-market environment. The buyer can acquire a property immediately at acquisition with a nice margin of safety, allowing them to purchase the asset for a much lower purchase price than the current market value. It's a win-win all around.

Most times, these non-broker types of deals are sourced by direct mail or cold call marketing campaigns. This is my personal favorite type of deal by far. Over 85% of our deals have been acquired off-market without a broker involved. Many sponsors who tout "off-market deals" are actually purchasing at-or-above market value—so most broker deals won't work for our model unless.

Deal Type #2: Seller Seeking Broker Opinion of Value (BOV)

This is where the seller is trying to hire a listing broker. This type of deal *can* be profitable—but in most cases, it's only mediocre due to the bidding war that often happens on the property. Let me explain.

Typically, a seller will call all the big brokerages to ask for a broker opinion of value (BOV) on the properties' resale value. Often, the conversation leads to the seller allowing the broker to share their deal with their preferred list of clients and ultimately try to bring an offer if that broker has a qualified buyer for their property. So the broker will call around to all their clients and peddle this "off-market listing", hoping one of them will buy. If one of their clients buy that asset, the broker will get a commission. Keep in mind, by this time, the seller is more than likely talking to five or 10 different brokers about their property—each of which have contacted their preferred list of five or 10 buyers. By the time it's all said and done, there are multiple bidders in a bidding war.

Deal Type #3: Seller Seeking Private Sale (Pocket Listing)

This is when a seller works with a broker, but wants to keep the transaction private. These are also called "pocket listings", which are usually the only good off-market deals that actually involve a broker. With these deals, for whatever reason, the seller doesn't want their property listed and plastered everywhere for the public to see.

This could be for many reasons. I've seen sellers who just don't want any touring of their property. Others don't want the broker to take their time to create a full broker package with the fear it will take a long time to list it—and they're in a liquidity crunch and want to sell fast. These sellers just want brokers to bring the best offer they can from the best buyers they can as quickly as they can.

When a seller brings this type of off-market deal to a broker, the broker will call just a few of their best clients and find one of them to buy. The only sponsors that get these types of off-market deals are repeat clients who bought from that broker before or have otherwise built a really solid relationship with them.

I experienced this sort of 'pocket listing' situation with an acquisition we had in 2017 in Salisbury, MD. Here are the details of that deal.

CEDARHURST & WALSTON MHP
Salisbury, MD | Off-Market Acquisition | Oct 2017

Overview

Cedarhurst & Walston MHPs are all ages, affordable communities totaling 180 spaces along Maryland's Eastern Shore. Both communities were acquired from long-time, legacy owners who developed the properties decades earlier and had kept lot rents at $250 for years, despite the fact that market rates were north of $400.

About the Project

Cedarhurst & Walston MHP were acquired through a pocket listing with a local broker. We'd been in contact with the owners for years but the family wanted to sell the asset via broker, so we nagged (politely) the broker for many months prior to the asset being listed to ensure we would be the preferred buyer.

The Challenge

Over time, the owners had become tired. When Sunrise took over management, **abandoned homes** were scattered throughout the community and the underground infrastructure was a mess. Both well and septic systems had deferred maintenance. Worse yet, abandoned homes attracted unruly residents and crime to the neighborhood. The poorly managed assets were also in need of general cleanup.

What We Did

Sunrise negotiated a combined $2.6mm purchase price for the properties. Upon acquisition, Sunrise replaced on-site management, pumped septic tanks, demolished unsalvageable abandoned homes, renovated salvageable park-owned-homes, and power washed units. Once aesthetics improved, Sunrise set about recapturing the loss-to-lease.

The Outcome

Sunrise grew the NOI substantially, ultimately increasing lot rents to just beneath the market rate. In June 2019, Sunrise executed a cash-out refinance on the property, returning all investor capital in the process. Investors now have an infinite cash-on-cash return while retaining equity in an asset that appraised for more than $6mm. All told, Sunrise **created over $3.5mm in sweat equity** within two years on an original investment of $1.1mm.

Deal Type #4: Seller Demands an Inflated Disposition Price (potential market deal)

This type of deal is not really a 'deal' at all. Sometimes, a seller demands a certain disposition price for whatever reason. Out of risk of embarrassment, no broker wants to list that deal on the open market at an inflated price—nor do they want to spend any time or money marketing the deal if they know it's not going to sell. So they call all of their worst clients—their most inexperienced and hungriest—to go try to find that deal and buy it from the broker. Needless to say, what they're really looking for is a sucker.

> **Most off-market deals brought to inexperienced buyers aren't *real* opportunities**

If a sponsor is asking you to invest in their first deal and touting that it's a high quality off-market deal, take that as a red flag. The bottom line is this: off-market deals presented to you (by someone other than the direct seller) can make for a good story, but not necessarily a good deal. When passive investment deals are presented to you, just know that when a broker is involved, the deal has more than likely had multiple bidders and will ultimately drive the price close to market price, even if those properties had been lightly marketed.

Creating Deal Flow: How To Source Deals

Knowing how to source good, quality deals is the key to ensuring you're creating consistent deal flow for your business.

Over the next few pages, I'm going to talk about some of my favorite methods for sourcing quality off-market deals. These methods will be your go-tos, as your business grows and thrives.

Commercial Brokers

When you're just starting out, it would be beneficial to have a solid commercial broker or agent in your court. Don't try to go it alone, especially not in the beginning. Look for someone who specializes in the asset class you're focused on—often a commercial broker is the expert in that class for their immediate area and beyond. This extended reach can be a major win for your business, as you'll have more help finding deals in and around your target market, and that meet your investing criteria.

Beyond just their reach, commercial brokers and agents have an intimate knowledge of that particular market. These are the people who sold literally *every* owner in that mobile park—and they know when each one plans to sell in the future.

Having these experts and teams work with you can be a major win and keep you in the know, short- and long-term. These brokers and agents have already done their homework—and *then* some. They have the relationships and they know every owner on the block—literally. That means when you want to buy, all they have to do is pick up the phone. And they will because, of course, real estate agents and brokers only get paid when they successfully connect the dots and drive a sale.

FIND AN EXPERT IN YOUR NICHE

No two real estate agents or brokers are the same, and that's a good thing. By specializing in specific asset classes, commercial brokers can help their clients find the perfect properties in their markets, leveraging their insider insights and relationships to move things forward.

When you're looking for niche agents and brokers, try a site like LoopNet. Search for commercial properties in your specific asset class and see who's selling. Then, simply pick up the phone and introduce yourself and your business model. Alternatively look at niche sites—www.MobileHomeParkStore.com, for example. Simply scanning for-sale and recently closed listings will give you a sense who controls that particular market. Start there and expand your connections.

A quick call to brokers or agents whose names you see over and over on these sites will likely turn up at least one or two willing to take on a new commercial investor. Soon enough, you'll have a rock solid contact list of industry connections by asset class, and you'll know exactly who to call when you're looking for your latest deal.

Agents and brokers are commission-based, so you may struggle to find a partner early on. In those early days, you're an unproven entity and, to the broker, that means you're an unknown when it comes to closing a deal and driving a commission check.

If you get initial pushback when reaching out to commercial agents and brokers, don't take it personally—but, also, don't expect to call a broker out of the blue and get their very best deals tied up with a bow. In the beginning, a broker will likely send you some less than optimal deals to see how you react—deals that are overpriced or, for one reason or another, have floated from investor to investor without a bite.

In these instances, that broker is simply looking for your reaction—your feedback to these bad deals. It's a test and they want to hear what you have to say. If you come back with smart, market-driven feedback, they'll know you're the real deal. If you don't, they'll likely walk. You want to be the investor who shines—you want this to be the first step in your broker relationship-building. Because often, if you successfully pass this test, they'll start sending you bigger, better deals quickly. If they see you "get it," they'll see you as a potential commission source and want to feed you these opportunities.

But at the same time, some won't. I've been in the mobile home park business for over a decade and we've purchased numerous properties with significant capital backing us. However, despite being a proven entity, there are plenty of brokers who won't give us the time of day. Why? Because they have 10 other buyers they've worked with for years or even decades—long before my team and I hit the scene. Working with us means sending fewer deals to their established buyer base—and potentially tarnishing those lucrative, long-standing relationships in the process.

Do yourself a favor and cast a wide net. Reach out to lots of commercial real estate agents and brokers. Network. Go to industry events and get in front of brokers you'd like to work with. Check in and touch base often. Soon enough, someone will toss you a good deal and, from there, you'll get more and more and *more* opportunities, rapid fire.

BUILDING BROKER TRUST

There's a broker I've known for more than a few years now, though we've never done a deal together. We've had dinner together many times and, often, spent time together at industry events, talking shop and getting to know each other and our respective businesses. I've spent money on him and he's spent money on me but there's never been a deal struck—we're both simply trying to build a relationship.

Broker/Buyer relationships go both ways—we *both* make money when deals happen.

This particular broker has been bringing deals my way for quite some time and, every time, I push back. It's become an ongoing joke between us—he brings me a deal and I say, "Look, you know I'd love to buy from you—but you also know your deals are just too expensive." And it's true. His deals make no financial sense for me or my business, so I never move ahead on one. I refuse to overpay, but I'm sure plenty of other buyers out there would.

I always end the call by telling him I hope we *can* work together soon—it keeps things upbeat and helps move the relationship forward.

Recently, though, he called with something interesting. He had an off-market mobile home park deal and he reached out immediately. This deal, I quickly realized, was priced right—and he'd offered it to me first since it's right near a pocket of mobile home parks we already have in our portfolio.

We've never done a deal together, but now we are. That's the power of relationship-building—he kept sending me deals and I kept reviewing them until, eventually, we found one that made sense for both of us. I suspect we'll be doing more deals over time—and I'm glad for it. But I also won't be afraid to say no when he drops something overpriced on my desk. Protecting my business is still my number one.

Direct-to-Owner Marketing

Going direct-to-owner is my all-time favorite method for acquiring deals and where the majority of my deals come from. Over the years, I've purchased office buildings, industrial spaces, mobile home parks and even a shopping center as a result of a direct mail campaign I ran. The reality is, you can buy virtually any type of commercial property using a direct mail or cold calling campaign as your jumping-off point.

Here's a recent acquisition that came as a result of a direct mail piece I sent out. I literally even flew across the country to break bread with the owner's family. Although the owner didn't make a move immediately, eventually he realized it was time to sell the community, and we got the first call.

CASE STUDY: DIRECT MAIL OFF-MARKET DEAL

RIDGEVIEW MHP

Lockport, NY | Off-Market Acquisition | Dec 2018

Overview

Ridgeview MHP is an all-ages, affordable community consisting of 146 spaces. The community was acquired in an off-market transaction, and sourced via our internal direct-to-owner marketing efforts.

About the Project

Upon receiving a direct mail piece, the legacy owner reached out to gauge our interest but was not quite ready to sell. Over three years, Sunrise continued to foster the relationship. Our lead principal, Kevin Bupp, even flew across the country to break bread with the owner's family. Eventually the owner realized it was time to sell the community, and Sunrise received the first call.

The Challenge

Touting a phenomenal school district and containing several high-end homes, Ridgeview MHP had good bones. The original developer held the park for decades, and ultimately became tired. When Sunrise took over management, pervasive potholes covered the roads, twelve vacant park-owned-homes needed renovation, and inflated expenses littered the financials. On the revenue side, average lot rents of $365 sat well below market.

What We Did

Sunrise negotiated a $3.86mm purchase price and began the turnaround by fixing the roads, renovating all vacant units, and replacing onsite management. Alluring landscaping was planted near the community's entrance to improve curb appeal, and new signage was installed to increase visibility. Lot rent leases on updated homes garnered the market rate of $480, boosting average lot rents in the community to over $400 while simultaneously increasing physical occupancy.

The Outcome

Sunrise substantially increased NOI, maximized the value of the asset, and created over $1.5mm in sweat equity within two years. With multiple unsolicited offers in a hot sellers market, we sold the asset in Q4 2020 and exceeded our targeted return for investors.

Direct Mail

Direct mail is, very simply, a letter, postcard or other mailer that is sent from you to your list—ideally, to potential sellers or buyers who may be interested in working with you. Think about each envelope, postcard or package like an extension of your team—they're like tiny salespeople, being sent into the market to pitch you and your business to sellers and buyers.

Again, the vast majority of commercial real estate deals happen off-market—they are not listed on Loopnet and the seller isn't broadcasting to the world that they're selling. It's a relationship game. If you have the right relationships with the right brokers—and those brokers have the right relationships with sellers and sellers' agents—then you'll have access to these valuable opportunities.

Direct mail is a great way to overcome those hurdles or, even, support the relationships you're actively building on your end and through your broker. Drop a direct mail campaign and you're creating one-on-one interactions with recipients, and attempting to take things to the next level—driving them to your website, to pick up the phone and call or to take some other meaningful action that pushes you toward a successful deal.

Even if you aren't a natural born writer, it's easy to master the format and the content basics of a direct mail campaign. All effective direct mail campaigns have four key elements:

1. They grab readers' attention

An easy way to grab recipients' attention is to use a handwritten envelope, a non-standard envelope or a combination of the two.

Compare this example to a more traditional, more formal envelope, and it's clear which is more likely to be noticed and opened.

If your direct mail piece isn't opened, it can't get your message across. So first and foremost, make sure you're drumming up attention for your direct mail piece from the minute the recipient sees it in their mailbox. Our most successful direct mail campaigns have had 10%-plus response rates, and it all started by getting the envelopes opened.

CREATING A CAMPAIGN THAT GETS OPENED

Beyond your envelope, consider the entire experience of receiving a direct mail piece. Consider using non-standard size paper, colored—or at least *non-white*—paper, paper with texture or designs and paper with other unique or attention-grabbing qualities.

We recently ran a direct mail campaign that used invitation-style envelopes addressed using blue ink. Inside, each letter was handwritten on legal paper using red ink. It was very simple, very low cost and took very little time—and we had a great response rate.

One of the sellers brought the letter he received to the close and spoke for several minutes about how compelling it was—THAT, he said, was what drove him to get in touch and, ultimately, to do business with us.

Taking a page from that successful campaign's playbook, we produced another campaign that also used a handwritten envelope. This letter was two pages and included a picture of my family—that definitely got attention, if nothing else. Other pieces have talked about my personal connection to and affinity for mobile home parks, for example. That often drums up attention with owners, who feel an instant connection to me and my business.

The takeaway: don't be afraid to change things up. Direct mail campaigns can and should be creative but, too often, become flat, boring and get lost in the shuffle.

2. They create an interest in you and your business

Like the envelope, every piece of your direct mail campaign should drum up interest among recipients. As you're assembling the actual mailing—the stamp, envelope, paper and any design elements—*and* as you're writing the copy, continuously ask yourself whether or not you'd be interested if YOU received and read this letter. If not, go back to the drawing board.

Focus on developing relevant written copy for each recipient. To do this, segment your list based on what you know about the seller recipients, then write copy that speaks to their unique pain points, challenges and goals. If you try to write generic copy that appeals to everyone on your list, you'll likely appeal to no one—it's the "jack of all trades, master of none" notion applied to direct marketing.

It's also important to write copy that shows you're in-step with the recipient in terms of values and interests. Again, I've written campaigns that focus on me, my family and our passion for mobile home parks. It's 100% true and 100% authentic, and I believe it shows in every direct mail piece I drop—and, more importantly, I believe that's why these campaigns have such strong success rates.

While you may not be so up-close-and-personal with every owner, chances are you know a few things—if they're a big business owner or if they're a mom-and-pop shop, for starters. Speak to owners through the appropriate lens and, chances are, you'll better engage recipients and drive them to take action—and get in touch with YOU to discuss next steps.

3. They build up a desire for added connection

We all want *something*—if you can hit on that person's wants, you'll immediately build desire and drive them to take action.

A good way to do this is to speak to a seller's pain points and position yourself as the problem solver. For example, if you know a seller is nearing retirement, your letter could speak to the challenges of managing properties from a distance—or the fact that they may be tired of managing a building after all of this time. While you don't want to harp or spend the entire letter unpacking pain points, mentioning them then presenting your value proposition could be a great way to add an important connection and level of desire.

When it comes to mobile home parks, we've often focused on the need for "discrete sales." Many mom-and-pop owners hold onto their parks for years—decades, even—despite not wanting to. They're exhausted, they're tired of the responsibility and they want out—but they also know others in the community may be disappointed or even angry if they sell. If you can articulate your understanding and your ability to be discrete, you'll likely appeal to those motivated owners who don't know what to do next—but know they want or need OUT.

4. They clearly ask for a 'next step'—for the reader to take action

All direct mail pieces should have a very clear call-to-action (CTA)—in other words, the specific next step you want them to take. In most cases, the CTA is simple—call to learn more, visit your website or send an email.

The specifics don't matter as much as how you communicate them—recipients should always know exactly what to do if they decide to move ahead, and should be able to take the next step *immediately*. If they have to read and re-read the letter to figure out what next or if they need to take multiple steps to engage, you need to re-work your call to action.

Cold Calling

Not everyone is going to respond to your direct mail outreach, and that's where cold calling comes in. Cold calling is a technique where you pick up the phone and call potential buyers or sellers and have a conversation with them to gauge their interest in working with you. Many times, I've sent a prospective seller direct mail and received no response—but then I pick up the phone, catch them at the right moment and have a deal on the table in no time.

This works both ways. There are plenty of people who don't want to be called or feel like it's intrusive. I recommend that you consider both direct mail and cold calling as an effective two-part approach to direct-to-owner marketing. You need both because you never know which marketing medium people will respond to. If you start with direct mail and layer in cold calling, then chances are, you'll strike up more than a few great deals.

Especially in the beginning, using a **cold calling script** is essential. Don't leave things to chance and don't assume you'll be a pro on the phone from day one. As you get better and better at making cold calls, you'll continue to refine your script and be able to go "off book" at some point soon. But for now, focus on perfecting your cold calling script.

All effective cold calling scripts begin with a "greeting."

Start every cold call sounding energetic, confident and natural, and keep that energy up throughout the call. No one wants to think the other person is reading a script, or spamming them.

In your Greeting, address your key points as quickly as possible—ideally in the first 5-10 seconds. Those points include: who you are, why you're calling, what you're hoping to accomplish with this call, and what action you want the owner to take.

Here's a good example of a quick, concise greeting. Imagine this being said with enthusiasm and confidence:

> *Hi, my name is Ashley with Sunrise Capital Investors. I'm calling in regards to the Mobile Home Park you own in Harbor Rapids. Did I reach you at a good time? Do you have a minute to chat about your park?*
>
> [OWNER SAYS "YES"]
>
> *Great! Our group is actively looking to purchase one to two mobile home parks in the Harbor Rapids market in the next few months and yours fits our general acquisition criteria based on its size and location. The owner of our*

company personally handed me your contact info and ask that I call you. Have you ever considered selling your park?

Ideally, the owner will say he or she is interested in selling, or would potentially be open to the possibility. Either way, you want to move them forward in the conversation. Confirm a time for the owner and "your boss" to speak. Some commercial investors use an assistant or VA to make these calls, while others are their own "assistant." Either way, schedule a time to follow up and discuss in more detail.

> *Great! What I'd like to do is set a time for you to speak with Kevin Bupp, my boss and primary decision maker in our company, so the two of you can have a lengthier discussion about this. How does 3:30 this afternoon work for you?*
>
> [SELLER SAYS "YES."]
>
> *OK, great! I have you on the calendar to speak with Kevin at 3:30 pm today, Friday the 18th. Do you have an email address where I can send a calendar invite and reminder for the appointment?*
>
> [SELLER GIVES EMAIL]
>
> *Perfect. Is this your preferred number for the call later today? 555-555-5555?*
>
> [SELLER SAYS "YES."]
>
> *Great! I'll also give you Kevin's direct number in case you need to reach him to reschedule. Do you have a pen and paper handy? Ok, his direct number is 555-222-2222. You can also learn more about our company at www. SunriseCapitalInvestors.com. Thanks again! I know Kevin is really looking forward to connecting.*

THE CASH FLOW INVESTOR

Of course, sometimes you won't get a "yes" or even a "maybe." Sometimes you'll get a flat out "no."

Objections aren't always cut-and-dry, even if they seem like it. Often, by better understanding where the sellers' "no" is coming from, you will be able to build a strong relationship with the owner and, eventually, move to a "yes."

Don't be shaken up or thrown off course by pushback or negativity. Instead, prepare for the most common objections and add to the list as you start cold calling. Eventually, when you hire an assistant, VA or cold caller to handle these calls for you, they will nee train them on what to say and when to say it—this list will be your jumping off point.

Common objections include:

- I'm not interested.
- I'm busy.
- I don't have time to deal with this.
- I need to talk to my spouse/co-owner/partner.
- I'm already working with a buyer.
- It's not for sale.
- I'm not interested unless you can pay... (insert exorbitant amount...)
- I'm not interested—try me back next year.
- HOW did you get this number??

The better rehearsed you are the easier it will be to recover from these objections. Jot down notes, test out responses and see what works. At the end of the day, people want to be heard. If you come at these calls

84

with their best interest in mind, you'll likely convert many of these "no" callers into deals down the road.

AN UNLIKELY CONNECTION...

Everyone responds to different methods of outreach differently. Personally, I would rather call someone after receiving their direct mail piece than be caught off-guard with a cold call—but, again, that's just me.

Recently, we made an interesting—and unexpected—connection. We've been mailing to a particular mobile home park for nearly four years with no response. One day, I received a call from a podcast listener. He knew the owner of this particular mobile home park and had just put it under contract. The only issue? He didn't want to buy it anymore.

During the course of our call, he offered to wholesale the deal to me. I checked out the aerial and realized it was the park we'd been mailing to for all this time. The original owner never would have responded—and, likely, wouldn't have responded to a cold call either. It took a slightly more roundabout path to get there, but we made the connection and closed the deal.

Networking

Networking is another excellent way to find deals. Go where the deals are. In other words, go to industry events where you can easily mix and mingle with the people who control the deals in your market. For example, I recently attended the Southeastern Conference for Mobile Home Owners and Operators. While this is a relatively small conference—about 200 to 250 people—the biggest brokers in this niche attend or send their teams. If you haven't connected with those power players, this is *the* chance—they're right there, front-and-center, waiting to engage.

Admittedly, I haven't done my part in engaging some of these experts—so this was my chance. I had coffee with one group, lunch with another and drinks with a third. Just making my presence known and creating those connections made the trip well worth it. Now, all I have to do is follow up and keep those relationships moving forward.

Every area of real estate investing has its own set of industry events and conferences, and each gives you an opportunity to network with the most important agents, brokers and decision-makers in your particular arena. Chances are, your market even has events, which can help you hone in on exactly who runs the market and who you need to get up close and personal with to ensure you're getting your share of the deals.

Granted, you won't always walk away from these events with a deal on the table—I usually don't. However, done right, these events are unparalleled opportunities to get face time with critical contacts while getting your name and business out there. That's important—getting your name out there, getting people to know who you are, and gaining trust is everything.

Collect a business card or contact information from everyone you meet and engage at any industry event or networking opportunity. Even if you don't hear from these new connections immediately, make a plan to check in once every two to three months—share updates about your business and your latest deals and see what they're up to and how, potentially, you can work together. In this business, you never know where your next great deal will come from, so it's important to keep engaging and keep *any* conversation alive, especially with fellow industry insiders.

Non-Event Networking

Don't simply wait around for the next big event. Networking can happen anytime, anywhere, even if there's significant distance between you and your core contacts. Simply hop online and check out websites like CoStar, LoopNet and the MLS—even social media sites like LinkedIn and Facebook can be valuable for tracking down active brokers, agents and investors.

Once you're online, see who's representing buyers and sellers for the kinds of deals you're looking for, then reach out and make the connection. Start with the brokers who have the most deals and listings—simply search for your market and your asset class and see whose name pops up over and over. It's not uncommon to see one name tied to 10, 20 or even 30 or more deals and listings in your asset class—start with them.

Again, brokers and agents are paid when they close deals. If you can show them you're deal-worthy, they'll gladly send opportunities your way.

Auctions

There are two ways to tap into real estate auctions to lock down deals. First, there's the more modern—and increasingly more common—approach: online auctions. Most advanced auctioneers will list their auctions on sites like LoopNet or CoStar.

However, more traditional auction houses still haven't shifted to digital. To get access to their deals, you need to be on their email lists.

To find commercial auctions, simply do a quick online search for "real estate auction houses" and "real estate auctioneers" and your market. Focus on auctions and auctioneers with minimally, a website—this shows they have some level of professionalism which you want in an auction house. In terms of online auctions, register with a few sites, including:

- www.Ten-X.com—the largest commercial real estate auction site in the U.S.

- www.Auction.com—offers both commercial and residential auctions.

- www.Tranzon.com—exclusively commercial, though listings are diverse.

Keep in mind most of these sites are very general—it's tough to find quality auctions that are strictly shopping centers or mobile home parks. Most are more generalized to commercial real estate as a whole, so be prepared to sift through deals that don't sync with your business plan. Good auction sites and auction houses are worth the time—get online, get on their lists and be sure you're staying on top of the latest opportunities. We recently bought a property from auction that came through Nationwide Auction House—we only knew about it because we were on their email list.

Commercial Listing Websites

While the majority of the best commercial deals are not listed and off-market, it's still important to make it a daily habit of looking online. There are countless commercial deals out there, and searching online, in combination with your broker connections, direct to owner outreach, networking and auctions, will ensure you're seeing everything that's out there—and that will ensure you're closing more lucrative deals and driving greater ongoing cash flow.

There are endless real estate sites out there and, chances are, you'll discover your own daily search approach based on your desired asset class or classes and market(s). These sites, though, are good destinations regardless of your search parameters. Start here and build out your must-search list, as needed.

LoopNet is one of the largest digital destinations for commercial properties. The website has more than 500,000 active commercial listings at any given time, including $240 billion in for-sale properties spanning more than five billion square feet. Major commercial firms including CBRE, Cushman & Wakefield, Century 21 Commercial and Newmark Knight Frank list here, so you're in good company.

CoStar, while not strictly a listing site, offers real-time commercial real estate intelligence that you can use to steer your investing and your business. Here, you can pull comparables with CoStar COMPS, analyze deals and better identify and gauge tenants.

CoStar Property Professional, like LoopNet, offers a fully searchable database of properties. Here, you can search by market and submarket, then immediately access photos, floor plans, stacking plans and more. The site spans office, retail, industrial and multi-family, ensuring you can find virtually anything you're looking for with a few quick clicks.

While there are deals to be had on LoopNet and CoStar, there's also a tremendous amount of competition—everyone can access the site and everyone does. If you aren't ready to move—and if you don't make searching the site a daily habit—you're going to miss out on opportunities. Some other websites to include in your daily "sweep" include:

- www.Crexi.com

- www.CityFeet.com/

- www.Ten-X.com

CASE STUDY:

BANK REO OFF-MARKET ACQUISITION: "BRING KEVIN A DEAL" REFERRAL

HURON ESTATES MHP

Cheboygan, MI | Off-Market Acquisition | July 2018

Overview

Huron Estates MHP is an all-ages, affordable community consisting of 111 spaces immediately juxtaposed to the local Wal-Mart. The community was acquired in an off-market, deed-in-lieu of foreclosure transaction.

About the Project

Sunrise received a tip from a podcast listener about a community bank that was interested in selling a non-performing MHP note. In order to take title to the property, we purchased the distressed note from the bank, inserted a court-appointed receiver, performed a deed-in-lieu on the note holder, and took ownership at a deep discount to market value.

The Challenge

Huron Estates experienced years of mismanagement and needed attentive care. A friendly community with fairly modern infrastructure and municipal utilities, the asset had good bones. But the former owner ran the property into the ground, operating at a **74% expense ratio**. Massive water leaks went months without attention, landscaping was unkempt, and potholes littered the pavement.

What We Did

Sunrise purchased the note for less than $1mm and began renovations by trimming overgrown trees, planting fresh landscaping, repairing damaged roads, rectifying deferred maintenance, replacing on-site management, stabilizing poor collections, and installing water meters to promote conservation. After significantly improving the community, Sunrise began billing residents for their individual water usage and moved lot rents to just below the market rate.

The Outcome

Sunrise increased the NOI, boosting revenue and lowering the expense ratio to 48%. Within three years, the **property value increased by 126%**. Having created significant sweat equity, Sunrise decided to sell the asset for $2.25mm, providing investors with an exceptional risk-adjusted return.

"Bring Kevin A Deal"

If you come across a property for sale or know someone who wants to sell, refer them my way! I buy deals nationwide and you can earn a pretty solid finders' fee for any off-market deal you bring that I close. Learn more: www.BringKevinADeal.com

CHAPTER 7
DEAL ANALYSIS

While commercial real estate investing is an exciting industry, it's important not to let your gut lead the way—that's a recipe for investing disaster. Think about your last non-related real estate investment. While you may have felt completely confident that the investment would pay off, did you ever really know? Sure, it may have seemed like a no-brainer—a company is on the rise, with a major influx of capital and some emerging technology about to dominate the market—but, at the end of the day, it's impossible to crunch the numbers and know exactly where your investment will land. Same goes for just about anything— even if you're a student of the market, it's tough to say with absolute certainty what is and isn't a "good" investment.

Not so, though, with commercial real estate investing. By analyzing potential deals with a few simple methods and calculations, you'll be able to walk into any opportunity knowing exactly where you stand and exactly what you are poised to gain. That's powerful and *that's* the foundation of a rock solid business and a rock solid financial future.

Being data-driven, to this extent, isn't just about crunching the numbers—though that's a big piece of the puzzle. Being a smart, strategic, data-driven investor also means pushing your gut aside and taking action based solely on the numbers. If the numbers—the cash flow, the opportunity, the upside—make sense, then you move ahead. If they don't, you move on to the next deal, no matter what your gut is telling you.

That's a tough thing for many commercial investing newcomers. However, as you get more and more comfortable with the deal analysis processes, you'll see how simple it is to determine whether or not you're getting a good deal—and you'll begin to see exactly how those good deals drive your business and your bottom line.

Being Data-Driven

From cash flow to economies of scale to the opportunity for major, ongoing paydays, there's a reason so many investors dive into commercial real estate investing. While the opportunities exist, simply signing on the line for a commercial property isn't a guarantee you'll find your fortunes. Far from it. To make money, you need to be strategic and data-driven. As we just discussed, if the numbers make sense, you move on a deal. If not, you walk away. Too often, though, new investors go with their gut and just gloss over the deal analysis piece.

Analyzing commercial deals is simple and straightforward—anyone can do it with a few basic calculations. Once you've mastered these equations, you'll be able to better understand the potential tied to any and every deal in minutes, so you can determine the best next steps and where opportunity truly exists.

One final note: while, at first, some of these approaches may seem in-step with residential real estate deal analysis, they're very different. When you invest in residential, you're investing in something completely different—different goals, different values and different approaches to understanding and analyzing what is and what isn't a worthwhile opportunity. Very simply, commercial drives more revenue than residential—a single-family home will almost always rent for less than a multi-family building or retail space, for example. Beyond that, commercial properties tend to have longer lease periods, adding another dimension—and difference—to commercial calculations.

While it may be tempting to apply residential analysis to commercial deals, it is the ultimate square-peg-round-hole scenario—and it's likely not going to give you an accurate assessment of any commercial investment opportunity.

Determining the Value of a Commercial Real Estate Investment

Commercial real estate deal analysis is simple and straightforward. If you can run some basic calculations, you can analyze any deal in any market, any time. That's powerful—*that's* what ensures you walk away with great properties that yield solid returns from day one. And *that's* what makes commercial real estate investors true successes in the short- and long-term.

Income Approach

While there are several methods for analyzing commercial real estate investment opportunities, the most common is an "income approach." An income approach can be applied to income-producing properties, and looks at the amount of income generated, plus a host of other factors, to assess how much that property could sell for right now, in the current economic climate.

When using an income approach, you'll look at the property's net operating income (NOI), sales of comparable properties (comps) and the capitalization rate. Additionally, investors should consider the property's current condition, as large-scale repairs and renovations can dig into immediate and future profits considerably. Beyond that, income approaches take into account average vacancies and property efficiencies—specifically, how efficiently a property is operating under the current management structure.

Within the income approach there are two core valuation methods:

1. The Direct (Income) Capitalization Method

2. Discounted Cash Flow (DCF)

Both approaches have unique advantages, disadvantages and use cases.

The Direct or Income Capitalization Method is the simplest approach to analyzing commercial real estate deals. To start using this approach, you must first calculate the NOI. NOI is the net income from a property for a given period, less operating expenses. To calculate the NOI:

Effective Gross Income - Operating Expenses = NOI

Keep in mind, NOI does not take into account capital expenditures, debt servicing and taxes.

You'll also need to calculate Capitalization Rate or "cap rate." A cap rate is the ratio of NOI to a property's value:

NOI / Value or Purchase Price = Cap Rate

In short, the cap rate represents the owner's ROI in a 12-month period, *before* capital costs, amortization, depreciation and taxes.

Once you've determined the NOI and cap rate, you can move into the property value calculation:

NOI / Cap Rate = Property Value

So, for example, if a property has an Effective Gross Income of $1,000,000 with $650,000 in Operating Expenses, the NOI would be:

$1,000,000 - $650,000 = $350,000

In this case, let's say the cap rate for a comparable property—or your desired cap rate—is 8%. Using this income approach:

$350,000 / 8% = $4,375,000

In this case, you can value the property at $4,375,000. If you can get it for $3,000,000, it's a steal. If they want $6,000,000, it's likely not worth your time to pursue.

An alternative income-based approach is the **Discounted Cash Flow (DCF) analysis**. When you use DCF, you're assuming the value of a dollar today is worth more than a dollar in the future. From there, the value of the asset in question is, simply, the sum of all future cash flows, discounted for risk. Riskier cash flow properties are discounted at higher rates, while more set-in-stone cash flow properties are discounted at a lower rate.

Because this approach takes into account future values, it's considered a very accurate way to calculate the value of commercial investments. To calculate:

DCF = CF1   + CF2   + … CFn

$$(1 + r)^1 \quad (1 + r)^2 \qquad (1 + r)^n$$

For example, if your goal is to generate a 9% rate of return, how much would you be willing to pay today for an investment which gives you back $100,000 each of the next three years? Your formula would be:

Present Value of Year 1 Cash Flow:

$100,000 / (1+ 0.09)^1 = $91,743$

Present Value of Year 2 Cash Flow:

$100,000 / (1+ 0.09)^2 = $84,168$

Present Value of Year 3 Cash Flow:

$100,000 / (1+ 0.09)^3 = $77,218$

By these calculations, the present value of all cash flows equals:

$91,743 + $84,168 + $77,218 = $253,129$

In other words, you would be willing to pay a price of $253,129 today.

HOW TO DETERMINE A PROPERTY'S VALUE USING DCF

To determine a property's value, factor in both annual cash flow and sales—i.e. terminal or residual value. Residual value is determined by looking at the prior year's NOI and dividing it by the future cap rate.

These aren't the only ways to determine intrinsic value. Some other common methods include the **Cost Approach, Sales Comparison Approach, Value Per Door** and the **Value Per Gross Rent Multiplier**. Depending on your specific scenario, one of these—or an income approach—will likely pop to the top in terms of use case.

Cost Approach

This method takes into account the cost to rebuild the property from the ground up—in other words, if you were to build this exact property from scratch in the current economy with the current cost of land, building materials, labor and rates, what would it cost you?

The Cost Approach is ideal when comps are tough to come by—perhaps, for example, the property you're looking at is very unique or has had some highly specialized additions or improvements over the years.

CALCULATION:

Value = Cost of Land + Cost of Construction - Appreciation

Sales Comparison Approach

This is also called the "Market Approach" and it relies on recent sales—comps—to determine a potential investment property's value. Using these comps, you work to figure out a fair market value for the property. If the 48-unit multi-family property sold for $2,000,000 three months ago, chances are your potential 48-unit investment property is worth about that much—provided, of course, other key details like condition, year built and amenities are similar or identical.

If comps are in-step with your potential investment property, you can still use the Sales Comparison Approach. Simply take the value of the comp property and add or subtract based on what your potential investment property looks like. For example, if your 48-unit building has a swimming pool, you might add $100,000 to its value. If it needs a new roof, you may subtract $100,000.

Value Per Door

If you're looking at a multi-door property—a multi-family property or multi-office commercial building, for example—you can use the Value Per Door approach to better understand the value of the property. This method assigns a set "per door" value and multiplies it by the number of doors in that unit. For example, that 48-unit building worth $2,000,000 would have a per-door value of $41,666.67. This is calculated as a consistent per door value, regardless of the size of the individual units.

CALCULATION:

Value = Value Per Door x Number of Doors

Value Per Gross Rent Multiplier (GRM)

GRM is used to measure and compare a property's potential valuation by dividing the price of the property by its gross income. This is a good method for identifying properties with low asks compared to market-driven revenue potential.

CALCULATION:

Value = GRM x Gross Rents

GRM = Selling Price or Value / Gross Rents

CHAPTER 8

PREPARING AND PRESENTING OFFERS

Making a deal isn't just about finding the property and crunching the numbers. It's also about getting the seller to see things from your perspective—specifically, that your offer is competitive and worth their time. If you can do that, you'll be able to successfully present countless offers, cutting through the clutter and minimizing negotiations. At this stage, that's always the goal.

Remember, offers should only be made when the numbers work. Real estate investing is not a gut-driven business but, especially in the beginning, it can be hard to separate your desire to move forward with a deal from the dollars and cents of it all. Do yourself a favor and, from day one, adopt a data-driven mindset. If the calculations and analyses we covered in the previous chapter indicate you have a good deal on your hands, then move forward to preparing and presenting an offer. If the numbers fall short of your wants, needs or expectations, walk away.

Not only are there endless opportunities for quality commercial investors, but there's also a good chance that whatever hurdle is standing between you and this particular property will disappear in the coming weeks or months. Often a seller recognizes the value you bring to the table and gets in touch, or the price drops considerably because, as you'd known all along, it was too high.

If you have to walk, don't completely close the door on the opportunity— but do keep pounding the pavement to find something that syncs. And when you do—whether it's your first property or your 50th—move into this step and prepare a compelling offer anchored in market conditions, property conditions and the seller's own unique motivations.

Three Signs it's Time to Present an Offer

Once you've completed your property and deal analysis, the next step is to determine if you'll be moving forward with an offer. Again, only move forward if the numbers align—in other words, if they meet these three criteria:

1. The property has a steady positive cash flow.

2. The property is stable or increasing in value.

3. The property meets your return criteria.

If you can answer "yes" to all three of these points, you're ready to move ahead in preparing and presenting a competitive, market-driven offer.

However, keep in mind you aren't buying a primary residence—you can't simply call your real estate agent and ask them to submit your offer. Making offers on commercial investment properties involves a few additional steps and several added layers. While they're fairly straightforward and easy to execute even if it's your first deal, it's important you follow this process to the letter.

This process will not only ensure your offer is presented in the best light, but it will help you get to "yes" that much faster—and, from there, start benefiting from the positive cash flow that comes with these investments.

Focusing on Seller Motivation

By this point you have a sense of the financials—what you should be offering and why. While that's essential to making an offer, there's another key piece of the puzzle that many investors overlook: the seller's motivation.

At this stage in your seller interactions, you'll have worked to understand that seller's motivation and why they want to unload the property. Now, it's important to use that information to construct a high-value offer that will, again, get you closer to a "yes."

Too often, investors give a price and, if they sense hesitation, they keep increasing their offer. That's problematic. Not only will you hit your profitability ceiling quickly, but you'll be showing your cards—specifically, that you could have gone higher and, likely, could go even higher from where you are now.

Beyond that, making real estate deals isn't always about the money. While you want to create cash flow and your seller wants to walk away with a hefty check, there's more to these deals than just how many zeroes. And that's where motivation comes in.

Understanding why the seller wants or needs to sell—their motivation— is central to making a compelling offer. When you understand why they're selling, you can prepare an offer that speaks to those specific needs or pain points. This, often, is more engaging and more enticing than the dollars offered.

For example, if you're dealing with a seller you know is inching towards retirement, they may be eager to move quickly and have this property out of their portfolio. This multi-family building or storefront could be the only thing keeping them here—the *only thing* standing between them and their ideal retirement.

Or maybe that retiree has another investment deal in the works that's more hands-off—an optimal passive cash flow vehicle to help them coast through their Golden Years. The problem? They need to off-load this property before they can invest in the new one. Again, the clock is ticking in both scenarios. The ability to close quickly would be an incredible win for this almost-retired seller.

In this example, if you could offer an expedited, all-cash closing, for example, your offer would seem extremely high-value—even if, let's say, you came in 5% less than the other offer. While that 5% matters, it likely doesn't matter as much as unloading this property in the next 30 days.

Speed isn't always the issue, though. Often a seller decides they want out of commercial investing and management—maybe they have a hefty portfolio of diverse properties and, now, want to shift their funds elsewhere. In many cases, these sellers wind up listing lots of properties at once, often in the same markets or with similar structures. And, often, that means there's a level of internal competition happening—an investor likely won't swoop in and scoop up multiple properties at once.

In this case, the seller's motivation is clear—they want out but there likely aren't enough buyers to get them off the hook in the timeframe they're looking for. Instead of making a "traditional" offer, you might suggest owner financing—the owner gets a monthly cash flow and isn't hit with capital gains tax, and you walk away with a premade portfolio of cash flow positive investment properties. Everyone wins.

These deals are common and, often, incredibly lucrative for the investor—but you have to know your seller's motivation before you can even attempt to structure a deal like this. Without knowing the retiree needed the money for another deal or that the portfolio holder was having a tough time selling *any* of their properties, it would have been impossible to structure these winning offers. Chances are, you would have gone in much higher and with much less value-add. Best case, you wouldn't get the deal. Worst case, you'd severely overpay because you didn't understand motivation.

HANDLING INITIAL OBJECTIONS

At this stage, it's not uncommon to get an initial seller objections surrounding:

- Due diligence
- Inspection
- Who pays closing costs and survey fees

No matter how these objections come in, plan to handle them verbally—via phone, ideally—before submitting an offer. Your goal should be to get *all* roadblocks out of the way so the only negotiations center on simple language tweaks and basic adjustments or add-ons.

Forget About the Future...

Another key piece is understanding what should—and shouldn't—be factored into the purchase price. In the prior chapter, we focused on deal analysis and the equations investors need to know to effectively and efficiently evaluate deals.

One of the considerations you should never make is future value. While you're likely planning to hold onto an investment property for the long-term, many new investors take into account what they anticipate happening when valuing a property—and that's a problem. Because if you base your offer on the idea that you'll grow monthly rents by 16% in the first three months and you *don't,* you've overvalued the property, overpaid for the property and, likely, lost money over these last 90 days.

If you're able to grow rent payments by 16% in the first three months, great—your cash flow will increase and you will have made a tremendous investment. However, if rents don't grow or don't grow by the double-digits you anticipated you've put yourself and your business in a bad place. In overvaluing a property, you're allowing your emotions and your ambitions to get the best of you, versus sticking with the data-driven course.

When making offers, only consider the here and now—the cash flow and opportunities tied to this property *today.* What the property is worth today is what you should pay for it today. There is no reason to compensate the seller for future improvement *you'll* make or future managerial issues *you'll* tackle. Pay them for their property and their work right now.

Besides the logic of it, if you're leaning on bank or institutional financing, you're going to have a hard time justifying a higher-than-appraisal offer—lenders won't usually allow buyers or investors to pay more than a property is deemed to be worth. So unless you want a major slow-down later in the process, stay the data-driven course and make an offer based on what a property is worth *right this minute.*

You will find people—agents, in particular—who will tell you not to evaluate a property based on current value and actual numbers. In their mind, you should look at pro forma numbers. Don't worry about them. Evaluate and analyze your deals based on right here/right now and go from there. If you've done your due diligence, you should go into the offer-making process confident and ready to negotiate.

Submitting a Letter of Intent

Now that you have the pieces in order—the deal analysis, the offer or range, the motivations and your due diligence backing it all—it's time to prepare a letter of intent (LOI) and kick off the negotiation process.

An LOI, as the name suggests, shows your interest in a property and your intent to purchase it based on the offer submitted. This letter comes before a contract is drawn up and signed. It will enable you and the seller to get on the same page and develop a mutually agreed upon purchase and sale agreement (PSA). Also, in working through the elements of the deal now, you'll save time and legal fees once the PSA is in play.

LOIs tend to be short—about two to four pages—and are non-binding. Plan to outline the major deal components only, including:

- Name of the property (if applicable)
- Property address
- Property tax ID number
- Legal description of the property
- Earnest money deposit amount

- Purchase price
- Payment arrangements (i.e. cash, mortgage, seller financing, etc.)
- Projected closing date
- Terms and timeframes for your due diligence
- Contract next steps—specifically, who creates and sends the PSA

You should also plan to include anything unique or particularly significant in the LOI—for example, if you've discussed the seller paying all closing costs or if there are environmental reports that need to be completed before a deal is confirmed, include that here.

Moving into the Purchase Agreement

Once the LOI is finalized, plan to move into your Purchase and Sale Agreement (PSA). While it's good to have a standard template for PSAs developed by your attorney, plan to customize each. No two deals are the same and, likewise, no two purchase agreements should be either.

As you're developing your purchase agreements, make sure you're always adhering to a few simple best practices:

- Always have an attorney write agreements.
- Always use an escrow agent for partnership funds.
- Always have an effective date in addition to the date the contract is signed.
- Always state in your contract that contingencies can only be removed in writing.
- Always indicate the owner pays utilities until the effective date—and that those utilities will be prorated.
- Always indicate property taxes will be prorated.

Any prorated fund—property taxes and utilities, plus any other unique expenses—should be held in escrow. Plan to hold a larger or non-prorated amount in escrow until those payments are due and made. After that, the remaining funds are returned to the seller. Ideally, include a simple clause in your agreements that states:

> *"In the event the taxes are reduced, the savings are given to the buyer. In the event the taxes increase while the seller still holds title to the property, the proration shall be adjusted according to the new tax amount."*

When you become a seller, reverse the clause to your benefit.

Letter of Intent Template

Download my Letter of Intent (LOI) template in the Resource Bundle I've included as a bonus in the back of this book!

Dealing with Seller Objections

Your goal is to streamline the agreement process as much as possible—that means dealing with seller objections before you move into the agreement stage.

Once the LOI and agreement are in play, it's not uncommon to get additional objections or concerns, even from the most motivated seller. Some common objections include:

Objection #1: Pricing Too Low

This is the most common seller objection. Even though you've come up with a market-driven price, it's likely much lower than the amount the seller had in mind. In these situations, be empathetic—remember, you're telling someone their property isn't worth as much as they think it is. That, for many, can be an emotionally-charged conversation—to them, you're devaluing the memories, the investments and the work tied to that property.

When you come up against this objection be kind, be empathetic, but be direct—this isn't a time for your emotions to take the wheel. Share your comps and how you arrived at your offer so the seller understands where the market is and what that means for their property.

What you *don't* want to do? Re-trade or renegotiate. This can make your offer seem like a low-ball, and can leave the seller with doubts about your authenticity and character—and that's never ideal when trying to finalize a deal.

As commercial investors we make our money on the buy—it's very different than residential investing. That doesn't mean you have to buy at a deep discount, but it does mean you have to make investments that make sound financial sense.

DEALING WITH A "LOW BALL" OBJECTION

Recently, we came very close to making an offer on a property—specifically, a portfolio of six properties in Topeka, Kansas. This broker rarely shares prices. Instead, he'll give all the financials and details for a property and hope the market responds and dictates a "fair" price. This approach is fairly typical in a seller's market, where there's more demand than supply.

Even though I know this is his go-to approach, I called him anyway and asked for a range. I had done some initial calculations and had a rough sense of where we needed to be, but there were several unknowns. I didn't want to waste the seller's time and I certainly didn't want to waste my own so I made the call—my goal was to get a ballpark and see if we were in the same general zone.

The broker agreed and shared his "ballpark"—about $15 million. At the time, I was in the $11.5 to $12 million range—clearly, we were off significantly. And, while I've seen asking prices swing $1 million or so, a $3 to $4 million swing wasn't going to happen. So I opted not to write an offer—the broker and seller understood where we were and why we were there, and no one's upset. If they change their mind, they know where to find us—and, maybe, we'll make an offer down the road if the properties don't sell.

Objection #2: The seller wants more earnest money down

To some sellers, the amount of earnest money you put down directly correlates to the quality of the offer—and the quality of you as a buyer.

If you find yourself in this situation, weigh your options. Ideally, you'll put as little as possible down—the money is "on hold" while in escrow, and isn't working for you or the seller. It's also refundable, so an increased deposit may make sense, especially if it's a nominal amount—or if you'd initially offered a truly bargain basement amount coming out of the gate.

Objection #3: They aren't really ready to sell...

If the seller pushes back but doesn't have a concrete reason, dig deeper—there's a good chance they aren't ready to sign on the line just yet. Often by scratching below the surface on these objections, you can get to the heart of the issue, and determine if there's anything you can do right now to keep the deal on track.

At the end of the day, though, if it's a timing issue—that, truly, they just aren't ready to sell right now—walk away, but plan to re-engage in six to eight months. Sometimes a few months—a few weeks, even—is all it takes for a seller to see what's out there and realize the value you're bringing to the table.

Objection #4: The seller needs the cash flow

If you're buying from a fellow investor, it's possible they suddenly get cold feet and worry about losing out on their cash flow, especially at this stage. Chances are, this monthly income plays a major role in their day-to-day, and by selling to you they're immediately eliminating that, and may wind up having to live on their savings. For some, that's a scary prospect.

Should you find yourself in this situation, be creative—seller financing, for example, could be a good solution, enabling you to take ownership of the property while still ensuring the seller has the monthly cash flow they're looking for.

Objection #5: The due diligence or closing time frame is too long

While we usually aim for a 45-day due diligence and 30-day close, be open to extending if need be. For example, it's not uncommon for us to push to 60-day due diligence if we can, or to push close to 45 to 60 days if the seller needs it. Again, it's about understanding motivation and how to get to close without adjusting your offer price. Sometimes chang your timeline can do just that.

On the other hand, some sellers want a quicker close—14 days, for example. If you know you can flip the property in that period, contact your attorney and get the contract in motion.

CHAPTER 9
DUE DILIGENCE & PRE-PURCHASE INSPECTION

If you've heard the old adage, "don't judge a book by its cover," you know this notion works both ways—don't assume a deal is or isn't good based on your initial impressions. That's where the due diligence and pre-purchase inspection phase comes in.

Even if you've done everything right—found an incredible deal, pulled relevant comps and run your numbers backward and forward, it's still essential to take a minute to dig into the due diligence process to ensure everything is as it seems. In other words, it's essential to dedicate time, talent and resources to the pre-purchase inspection process no matter what.

Even if you think you know everything about the property.

Even if you know the property has extreme rehab needs.

Even if it's a new build.

Even if you know—and trust—the current owner.

No matter what the circumstances surrounding the deal are, you need to do your due diligence and you need to do it well. Because this critical step is, often, all about expecting the unexpected. The perfect investment property can be silently harboring major issues that could derail your deal or keep you from being profitable in the short- and, even, long-term.

The due diligence process isn't just about spotting structural issues with a property. During the due diligence process, you'll also verify cash flow, tenant quality, expenses and other bottom line cash flow considerations that, again, could derail or support your deal.

Like a major roof leak or massive plumbing problem, you don't want to wait until you've signed on the line to find out your new tenants are delinquent in their monthly rents, or that the majority are moving out at the end of their lease.

Due diligence and thorough pre-purchase assessments are essential—never skip and never cut corners. Understanding exactly what you're getting into before you ink a deal will ensure you're always moving forward with opportunities that make sense—opportunities that will drive positive cash flow from day one or, at the very least, have needs and challenges that you're aware of going in, so you can structure the sale accordingly.

Typical Timeframes For Due Diligence

While no two deals are the same, assume most can—and should—operate with a 30-60 day due diligence period built in. This will be clearly outlined in your purchase and sale agreement so both parties understand the expectations, timing and what needs to happen during this inspection period.

To ensure you can accomplish everything you need to do in that relatively short window, it's essential to plan the work and work the plan. You need to be organized, deliberate in your next steps and committed to following each step in the process as it's laid out. Start skipping steps or glossing over inspection points and you could wind up closing on a less-than-optimal deal.

REASONS NOT TO EXTEND YOUR DUE DILIGENCE WINDOW

Some sellers—especially relatively new property owners—may be open to extending the due diligence period. It's always good to push closer to the 60-day range when negotiating, especially if you aren't in a rush to close. However, don't get in the habit of pushing too far outside that window. While a seller may be open—or it may be necessary, under certain circumstances—asking for lengthy due diligence periods can make you look like a less serious buyer.

Remember, the due diligence period comes with an out clause—if you unearth major issues or other costly considerations during this process, you can walk away from the deal, penalty-free.

What to Do During the Due Diligence Period

Again, the due diligence period is about just that—doing your due diligence and confirming an investment deal makes sense. During this window, you'll want to check and recheck everything including:

- The property and property fundamentals
- Income, expenses and cash flow
- Financing, if applicable
- Environmental reports
- Surveys
- Compliance and legal obligations
- Any potential issues emerging, such as zoning problems, titles and liens

Additionally, if you haven't already had a professional property inspector survey your potential deal, this is the time. While you've done walkthroughs at this stage—and while sellers are legally required to disclose certain issues such as restrictions, easements and encumbrances— it's essential to do your due diligence and double check.

During a professional property inspection or a follow up walkthrough during the due diligence period, you'll be able to spot anything that was missed initially. Not only will this confirm you know what you're getting into by moving to close but, should something new emerge, you'll have the opportunity to walk away or, potentially, gain negotiating power if you decide to go forward.

This is a good time to confirm that your end goals align with the property specifications. For example, if you plan to convert a building into an office space, ensure there's enough parking—or could be enough parking—to accommodate tenants. If you plan to open a senior center, be sure the property isn't too hilly or tough to navigate for people in wheelchairs or walkers.

Likewise, use this time to confirm your intended use syncs with any necessary local, state and federal guidelines and regulations—that, for example, you can build that shopping center or subsidized housing and that there are no mandates that preclude you from moving forward. It's not uncommon for a community to have regulations around commercial development. It's better to find out you can't open a shopping center or convert a building into low-income housing *before* close, than after.

Verifying Income and Expenses

In addition to confirming the state of the property, spend time verifying income and expenses. To do this, you'll need to pull a series of financials that, together, confirm income and costs tied to the property. From there, it's easy to determine and verify your anticipated cash flow now and in the future.

Verification Documents Needed:

- Complete, executed copy of every lease agreement and guaranty, plus amendments issued

- Certification and confirmation there are no other leases—verbal or otherwise—circulating

- Certified rent roll

- List of all other income—for example, parking income, revenue generated from laundry rooms, etc.

- Recorded security deposits, plus all terms and refund stipulations

- Common area maintenance costs, broken down by source and payment schedule

- Two to three years of maintenance and utility fees
- All active service contracts, plus service contracts expired in the last 12 to 24 months
- Three years of real estate tax bills, including assessments, incentives, grievances, protests and any other relevant documentation
- Real estate tax contributions by tenant
- Three years of tax statement, insurance policies and warranties
- Schedule of any active or pending litigation or pending claims against the building/management
- ADA (Americans with Disabilities Act) compliance documentation

Once you've received these documents, spend time reviewing each. It's essential to thoroughly review lease payment histories to confirm a predictable rental income flow—typically, this is the foundation of your investment property's cash flow.

Also, be sure to scrutinize all financial records and operating statements, looking specifically for gaps in lease payments and other income-producing sources. If you spot something, ask. Post-close it may be too late to course correct.

TITLE SEARCHES & ASSESSMENTS

Once escrow is opened, be sure to order a preliminary title report. The title will provide information about the property, including previous ownership, lien history, encumbrances and easements. In conjunction with the survey, you'll be able to confirm everything from boundary lines to lot size and more. This will also ensure there are no title issues that could keep you from closin

Third Party Reports Needed During Inspections

Beyond inspections and financial evaluations, you'll also need to pull environmental reports and surveys. If you're financing your investment deal, this is required. Lenders almost always require environmental suitability assessments. But even if you're working with a private lender, partner or personal capital, it's important to follow through with, minimally, a Phase I Environmental Site Assessment (ESA).

A Phase I ESA is a deep dive into a property's history to confirm key details that could impact is suitability and usage. For example:

- What was previously on this site/property?

- What was the past usage of this site/property?

- Were any contaminants used previously that could impact the soil, water, air or surrounding areas?

- Are any hazardous materials or chemicals used onsite?

During this process, a qualified environmental engineer will assess these past and current usages based on onsite inspections, aerials, photographs and fire insurance mapping. This often requires that your engineer pull government environmental records to confirm any spills, harmful emissions and/or hazardous material manifests.

Once the Phase I ESA is complete, you'll receive a complete report of findings along with recommendations for further Phase II investigations, if needed. If no major issues are uncovered, no recommendations will be included and the assessment is considered closed.

Ultimately, the goal of these ESAs is to protect you from making a bad investment deal or, in the future, becoming liable for related issues on your property. Even if a property seems "clean" and environmentally sound, don't ignore this essential step. Often the biggest issues with investment properties are what lies below the surface—in this case, literally.

Pulling Surveys

It's essential to pull surveys for your potential investment properties. Again, the biggest issues with investment properties often come from issues lying below the surface. Like a Phase I ESA and mechanical inspection, a survey can help to suss out issues before they become costly liabilities.

When you perform a survey on a building or piece of land, you'll confirm any potential complications and, ultimately, if this property is truly viable and is poised for profit.

During the survey process, you'll get a full assessment of the land and related buildings. You'll also have the opportunity to dig into easements, defects, complications, contaminants and property-based conflicts— borders and boundaries, for example.

Legally there are even more reasons for surveys. In drawing up surveys, you'll better understand borders and concerns over natural phenomena like flooding and earthquakes. Beyond that, though, you'll walk away with a clear-cut document that outlines borders—borders between your property and adjacent properties, specific areas designated for features like parking lots, green spaces and more.

Typically, though, the most common purpose of surveys is to determine borders and boundaries. Legal descriptions of properties may or may not sync with the deed or boundary lines created down the road. As a result, conflicts can easily arise—a survey immediately resolves all boundary lines.

For most commercial investors, this is where the bulk of the hard costs come in. You'll be able to conduct most due diligence on your own, with support from your team. However, the survey, environmental reports and mechanical and structural inspections should be handled by a professional.

HANDLING MECHANICAL & STRUCTURAL INSPECTIONS

At the very least, plan to have a basic mechanical and structural inspection completed during the due diligence phase. This should include a professional inspection of key elements in the property that could be expensive to repair or replace and could impact whether or not you move forward with the deal.

Mechanical inspections should include:

- HVAC
- Boiler
- Roof
- Electrical
- Plumbing
- Foundation
- Anything property-specific that would be considered a "major" repair or rehab project

If you or your inspector spots anything mechanical or structural during the due diligence, don't simply move forward blindly. Instead, review your calculations, your offer and determine if it makes sense to move ahead—and, if so, what terms need to change.

There's no set hard cost for these elements—it all depends on the size and scope of the investment property as well as the market you're investing in, timing and professionals selected. Your real estate agent or broker can help you plan for these added costs on a case-by-case basis.

CHAPTER 10

PUTTING TOGETHER YOUR DEAL STRUCTURE

Like anything, it's essential to have the right framework in place before diving in—that's where this chapter comes in. Here, you'll learn how and why to create individual legal entities for each of your commercial real estate investments, as well as for your "core" business.

If you think this chapter doesn't apply to you—your business is too new, too small or still just a *concept?* Think again.

The minute you start investing in real estate, you need to understand the legal ramifications, and how these structures can protect you, your family and your *other* investments. If someone slips and falls walking into your multi-family investment building and you *don't* have the right corporate structure in place? The lawsuit that ensues could not only impact your financial interests tied to *that* property but, also, your entire portfolio and your *personal* assets. That's something you want to *avoid.*

That's exactly the bullet you dodge when you create individual entities for your investment properties. By creating this cut-and-dry structure for each, you avoid any interests—or finances—overlapping. What happens to or with one investment is limited to that property only, and that's key to safeguarding your interests and your long-term wealth.

Beyond that, there are lots of benefits to proper deal structuring, from ownership transfers to flexibility in shares to tax breaks. The core message is simple: each deal needs to be its own legal entity to protect you, your business, your investors and your portfolio.

Separate Legal Entities Protect Your Interests

When you start a real estate investing business, a big part of that is the structure of your organization. Depending on your unique products, services, goals and existing structure, you can opt for a host of different legal formations, including limited liability companies (LLCs), S-Corporations, nonprofit corporations or even sole proprietorships, among others.

However, if you're investing in commercial real estate, your entity creation shouldn't stop there. Each individual commercial investment you make—every multi-family apartment building, every shopping center, every piece of raw land—should be established as its own entity separate from your "core" organization.

That is something new real estate investors often overlook—and that's a problem. By creating individual entities for each of your investment properties, you're safeguarding the others—and yourself—through added asset protection, more favorable tax structures and decreased liability exposure.

Each time you create a separate legal entity, you're essentially drawing a line around those specific assets and liabilities—everything is 100% confined to that property and that investment.

While that may not seem like a major benefit at face value, the implications are significant and substantial. Even though each of these business structures will roll up to you and your core business, having unique entities established keeps challenges contained within the individual property.

For example, if your apartment building is dealing with a lawsuit, the judgment will never be able to touch your shopping center and office space. In the eyes of the law and the government, these are separate businesses. An issue with one *only* impacts that one—the influence ends there. This is known as "corporate veil" protection.

By establishing separate entities, you're also protecting *those businesses* from your own personal finances—this is called "charging order" protection. In these scenarios, if you've been charged with personal liabilities, creditors won't be able to go after your commercial investments, provided they're established as individual entities.

A good example would be a major judgment, like a lawsuit or bankruptcy. If you were to declare bankruptcy or be ruled against in a lawsuit, you would be personally liable, but your entities would be safe—no one could take them or pull from these profits.

Entity Formation

Many investors opt to form individual LLCs for each of their commercial properties. These legal entities get a tax identification number (EIN), making each one "officially" a business. Once you've formed an LLC, you're no longer personally responsible for any liabilities created by the entity—hence the name "limited liability" company.

That's just the beginning of the benefits for commercial investors. LLCs receive a host of tax benefits including:

- Pass-through taxation: acquire property through an LLC and you'll avoid double taxation. Any income and capital gains generated through your LLC pass through to you, the owner— but you only have to pay taxes as an individual. It's a win/win— you're treated as an individual for tax-paying purposes, but have no personal liability for your LLC.

- Versatile management structures: corporations have concrete structures and rules governing how roles and responsibilities are assigned—not so with LLCs. Within an LLC, you can personally manage the entity as the owner, or can tap another individual or third-party. The choice is yours.

- Lower fee structures: Many states charge corporations fees based on the number of authorized shares it has. While LLCs will still have to pay if they exceed a certain number, those fees tend to be much lower, as are state registration and maintenance costs.

- Better profit distribution options: S-Corporations, for example, require pro rata cash flow distribution—not so with LLCs. LLC members can be compensated and financially rewarded based on anything from upfront investments to sweat equity.

- Simple ownership transfer: Once established, it's very easy to transfer ownership of an LLC. Holdings can even be "gifted" to people without a full-on deed. Not only is this easy, but it can help the recipient avoid certain taxes and fees.

Alternatives to LLCs

While LLCs are the most popular structures, you also have the option of starting individual C-Corporations (C-Corps) or S-Corporations (S-Corps) for your investments.

C-Corps are standalone legal entities that, like LLCs, protect owners from liability—to a point. In these structures, owners are personally liable for the amount they've invested in the corporation. Beyond that, they're exempt from liability.

As a C-Corp owner, you can be a manager or a passive investor, and there's no limit to the number of shareholders your corporation can have at a given time—and to transfer ownership, all you have to do is sell your shares. These corporations are subject to both corporate and income tax.

S-Corps are also legal entities but, unlike C-Corps, S-Corps are treated as a pass-through for tax purposes. However, they are not subject to double taxation.

Sole Proprietorships are the most basic type of business. As soon as you start a small business or start performing services as a freelance, consultant or contractor, for example, you're a sole proprietor. Because this isn't an "official" business, there's no separation between you and your company. You're liable for anything that happens or any debts owed. You'll also declare and personally pay all taxes associated.

Understanding Partnerships

Unlike LLCs or other corporate structures, you also have the option to create a partnership. Like sole proprietorships, partnerships are simply extensions of the owner—in this case, you.

Because of this structure, partnerships are eligible for pass-through tax benefits—you, as the owner, will be accounting for the business income and expenses on your individual tax returns. However, partnerships aren't separate legal entities like LLCs. As a result, you and your personal assets—and other sole proprietorships and partnerships—aren't protected from liabilities.

Partnership structures don't receive the same level of tax considerations as LLCs. On the flip side, though, partnerships are extremely flexible—there are no concrete requirements when it comes to management structure, payout or ownership changes.

As a result, these tend to be a default business structure. When a business owner or commercial investor does nothing, they often wind up rolling into a sole proprietorship or partnership because of the ease factor.

Structuring The Right Teams and Partnerships

Beyond just your corporate structure, it's important to structure the right team to manage and oversee your corporation. This team should be comprised of individuals and vendors or partners who, together, can help you find, secure, close and manage your commercial properties—essentially, everyone you need to do your job *right*.

Keep in mind, not all of these team members need to be full-time or even employees. Especially in the beginning, you'll likely want to bring on freelancers, contractors or other part-time professionals to help grow your business. Eventually, if your needs demand, you may opt to create a team of full-timers—or you may opt to keep a more flexible team structure.

Regardless, you'll need to find the right talent to help your business excel.

Commercial Real Estate Broker or Agent

As I talked about earlier, a skilled commercial real estate broker or agent can be extremely valuable to your business. Look for someone who specializes in the area you want to invest in. This isn't the time to rely on someone else who's just learning the market, too.

You need someone who has connections and can get deals done. Remember, the majority of commercial deals never hit the market, so having a top-notch broker or agent with access to these opportunities is critical to your business' success, now and in the future.

Mortgage Broker

Even if you plan to fund your deals alone or with an existing partner, it's a good idea to have a mortgage broker in the wings. When you need funding, your mortgage broker can help connect the dots, and find the right lender for your investment goals and financial profile— and they can even help package and present you to that lender to better your chances of securing the funds. Some mortgage brokers even fund deals themselves, which could mean an added funding source for your business.

Real Estate Attorney

Your attorney will be central to launching and scaling your business, from helping you structure your initial corporate entity to drafting go-to agreements, addendums, contracts and more. You'll also need to work with your attorney on every transaction, to ensure your interests and funds are protected.

Be sure to work with an experienced real estate attorney. While any lawyer can, technically, help you with your immediate needs, be sure you're dealing with someone who has concrete (and current) experience, versus someone who's learning as they go. The documents and structures your lawyer puts into place will be central to your business operations now and in the future—that's something you can't and shouldn't risk.

Bookkeeper or Accountant

Owning a business has many tax implications—so does investing in commercial real estate. Together, owning a business that invests in real estate weaves a very complex web that can be confusing and costly if not managed properly. Be sure to have a professional on board, from day one, to manage everything from taxes to lease payments to budgeting and payroll.

Insurance Agent

Every property will require very specific insurance—and, often, those policies need to be turned around very quickly. Having a trustworthy insurance agent on board will help you get premium quotes on-demand, then lock down the policies and renewals you need going forward.

This will help protect your property, your tenants and your long-term interests. Eventually something *will* go wrong, and having the right insurance on the right terms will enable you to move forward.

As your investing business grows, you'll likely want to add other professionals such as cleaning crews, electricians, contractors, handymen, plumbers and painters—all experts who can help you get properties up and running, and managed properly.

Creating A Team Banks Will Endorse

In structuring your team, you're setting yourself up for success—anytime you're ready to move on a deal, you'll have the people you need ready to finalize things and help you start driving a positive, productive cash flow.

That is just one of the benefits. As you start presenting your deals to partners, sponsors, banks and lenders, you want to show you're established and trustworthy experts—people they should want to do business with. While selling yourself, your creditworthiness and your profit potential is good, showing that you have experts backing you up every step of the way is even better. That's where your team comes in.

CHAPTER 11

FUNDING THE DEAL

One of the most common misconceptions in commercial real estate investing is that you need tons of cash to invest. The reality? While funding needs to come from somewhere, it doesn't need to come from you, personally. It's great to have some working capital on-hand and, in some cases, you'll need to show that your net worth at least partially supports a loan request. But, at the end of the day, you're going to primarily use other people's money (OPM) to close your commercial deals.

If you're new to commercial real estate investing, it's important to remember the funding process *is not* the same as it is in residential investing or home buying. Many people assume getting a commercial loan is like getting a home mortgage—just that much bigger and more complex.

In some cases, it's true. If you opt for more traditional bank lending, you'll likely follow a more structured path to secure funds—a path that includes pulling credit reports, financial statements, business plans, tax records and other essential documents and insights.

However, banks and traditional lenders aren't your only option. As a commercial investor, you can pull funds or create customized funding structures from just about anywhere, creating unparalleled value for you, your business and your seller while, at the same time, enabling you to grow your portfolio regardless of your personal or corporate capital.

Funding Deals With Banks And Traditional Lenders

If you're looking for more structured and traditional funding—which many commercial real estate investors are—banks and lenders are likely a good source. Within this landscape, you'll find six core types of loans:

1. Small Business Administration (SBA) 7(a) Loans
2. Certified Development Company (CDC)/SBA 504 Loans
3. Conventional Loans
4. Commercial Bridge Loans
5. Hard Money Loans
6. Conduit Loans

Depending on your unique circumstances and timing, one or more of these loans will likely make sense for your latest investment. Each, though, has its own set of eligibility requirements—be sure you understand what's needed and whether you qualify before starting the process.

Working with a bank or traditional lender tends to follow a very similar and straightforward process.

Step 1: File as an individual or entity

In the previous chapter, we discussed creating individual legal entities for each of your commercial investment properties. If you've done that, you can file for a commercial real estate loan as an entity. If not, you'll need to file as an individual.

Keep in mind, most commercial real estate is secured by businesses, corporations or other legal entities—considering the hefty price tags on many commercial buildings, that shouldn't be a surprise. However, banks and lenders will consider individuals and sole proprietors. If you opt to go this route, it's especially important you have a solid team in place, as discussed in Chapter 9.

Regardless of how you file, the bank or lender will be looking at the same thing: your ability to pay back the loan. If you're a first-time investor or if you file as an entity with no background or history of successful loan repayment, you'll likely need a guarantor—investors to back you or a partner with a more established history.

Step 2: Understand your loan options

Again, there are six core types of commercial real estate loans. While bridge loans are *very* short-term—usually a few months to a few years—the others tend to have terms from 5-20 years. Unlike residential mortgages, these loans are not backed by government agencies and typically come with higher interest rates.

Step 3: Determine your loan to value (LTV) ratio

Your loan to value (LTV) ratio determines the value of your loan against the property value—in other words, what percentage of the property's value does the loan make up. In commercial deals, banks and lenders will typically approve LTVs in the 65%-80% range. The lower your LTV, the better your terms and rate will likely be.

Step 4: Assess cash flow

Banks and lenders also want to understand the debt-service coverage ratio (DSCR). This measures a property's capacity to service a debt, by looking at annual net operating income against mortgage debts, including principal and interest accrued. Most banks and lenders aim for DSCRs of 1.25% or more to ensure there's a solid cash flow—less than 1% signals a negative cash flow—and the inability to repay the bank.

Ultimately, banks and lenders are looking for solid deals—if yours will clearly produce positive cash flow and your plan for creating that cash flow is solid, you'll likely get the loan. However, expect to be scrutinized, especially if it's your first deal—banks and lenders don't like to foreclose on properties or have those REOs on their books. By confirming you're a responsible borrower personally and professionally, they're increasing their chances of being paid back—with interest.

Using Private Money To Close Deals

Many commercial investors don't always go the bank route. Many tap into private money resources to secure very favorable rates and repayment structures, all while securing the cash they need to close the deal.

A **private money loan** is a loan and other funding that comes from anyone outside of a traditional banking or lending structure. Some private money lenders do this full time, alone or with a group of private lenders. Others invest in one-off deals from time to time—or, maybe, even once—because they see the value in commercial real estate investing.

Because of the relatively loose structure of private lending, *anyone* can be a private money source if they're putting up their own cash or capital to fund a deal—your mother, father, sibling, cousin, spouse, neighbor, former colleague... it doesn't matter. And, because these loans come from private lenders, those lenders can determine the terms, repayment structure and other requirements like LTV and DSCR.

Private lending is a great go-to for any commercial investor, but tends to be particularly valuable when investors are just starting out. Because there's no set framework, a private lender can offer very low interest rate—even a 0% rate—or provide a payment-free period for the first few months. Private lenders may also be willing to fund the entire deal versus 65%-80% and, potentially, the renovations and rehab work you'll be tackling. Again, because there's no formal governance over private loans, it's all up to you and the lender.

Be sure you're getting *everything* in writing—your attorney can help with that. Just because these loans have a looser framework doesn't mean there should be *no* rules or parameters. Be sure both sides are clear on the exchange, then move forward. Some private money lenders may even become partners down the road, creating a more consistent funding source while helping your private lender benefit even more.

Securing Deals Through Syndication

Within the private money scope, another good option for commercial investors is to fund deals through syndication. When you use syndication, you're essentially *crowdfunding* your deal, pooling resources and funding from a variety of individuals or organizations. The central tenet of syndication is simple: you, the investor, have the knowledge and your investors have the cash. Together, you can get the deal *done* and the cash flowing.

Though terms can vary, most commercial investors aim to invest 5% to 20% of their own funds—depending on deal size—then leverage syndicated investors for the remaining amount. Each investor has a "preferred return" rate which they're paid annually, usually about 6%-8%.

In addition to preferred returns, investors in syndication also get a portion of the profits once all payments are made. For example, if you have a 75/25 profit split with your investors, they would get 75% and you would get 25% of profits. That 75% is split among the investors based on the amount of their upfront investment.

WHAT A SYNDICATION DEAL LOOKS LIKE

Let's use the 75/25 example from above. This profit split structure means:

- Your investors get 75% of profits, split amongst themselves based on their individual investments.
- You get 25% of profits.

If you have $1.5 million in profits with 25 investors each contributing equally, your profit split would look like this:

- Your profits: $1,500,000 x 25% = $375,000
Investor profits: ($1,500,000 X 75%)/25 = $45,000 per investor

Keep in mind, to syndicate deals you'll first need to establish an LLC or Limited Partnership (LP) and designate yourself the "Sponsor" and General Partner or Manager. Your investors will then become limited partners or passive members. All rights and distribution information should be spelled out in your Operating Agreement if you're an LLC or

Partnership Agreement if you're an LP. Your attorney can work with you on these documents, as needed.

Integrating Owner Financing

Owner financing is another non-bank alternative, ideal for new commercial investors. In these structures, the seller becomes the bank— and like private money lending, they can dictate the terms, interest, repayment structure and more.

Owner financing is a good option when the owner is reluctant to give up their monthly cash flow or when you're concerned about securing traditional financing because of limited capital or a less-than-ideal credit history. It's also a good approach for sellers who want to avoid a major capital gains payment, or who want to minimize their reportable income in the short-term.

As the buyer, you'll also benefit. Again, if your credit or experience level is less than optimal, you may have a better time working with a seller to structure a deal versus a traditional bank or lender. This will also bring down many upfront costs typically associated with commercial borrowing, helping you create greater cash flow even sooner. And because these deals aren't reported to credit bureaus, you'll keep your credit clear for future borrowing.

CHAPTER 12

MANAGING YOUR INVESTMENT

Closing deals and building your portfolio is just part of the journey. You aren't just a passive investor putting down cash to get a piece of the earnings. You are the investor—you're the person leading the charge and driving the cash flow. That means effectively and efficiently managing each property for the long haul. As a long-term real estate investor, you need to be adept at managing those properties—that's what we'll examine in this chapter.

There are a number of ways to effectively, efficiently manage your portfolio—some more hands-on than others. Depending on your goals, your experience and your overarching investment strategy, you may want to personally manage the properties yourself, or you can hire an outside management company to keep the trains running.

There's really no right or wrong answer when it comes to managing properties. The choice is yours and, ultimately, should come down to your available time and overarching goals. If you have the time and bandwidth, and if managing properties fits with your cash flow objectives, it could be the right next step. If not, it may be time to hire a pro. Either way, it's essential to put your properties in the right hands and, from there, to ensure they're well-managed, well-maintained and producing maximum returns month after month.

Managing Your Own Properties

Many investors opt to manage their own properties if they have a smaller operation—for example, if they have a few single family home rentals, multi-family property or two or, even, a smaller apartment building. If this looks like your portfolio, or if this is where you see yourself going in the short-term, then in-house property management may be your best bet. Chances are, your management needs will be fairly basic—collecting rent, replacing light bulbs in common areas, maintaining communal spaces, landscaping and other fairly straightforward tasks.

Granted, even in these instances, that doesn't mean you have to personally manage every aspect of property management. While, yes, you would have to oversee the work and maintenance get done, many property owner/managers don't roll up their sleeves and scrub landings or mow lawns. If time prohibits, or if you simply aren't handy, then consider hiring professionals to fill the void.

For example, you could hire a landscaping company to keep up with general outdoor maintenance, including snow-shoveling in the winter. You could tap a cleaning company to clean common areas throughout the week. You could even hire a local handyman to answer tenant requests. This leaves your job to simply ensure these professionals stick to a schedule and keep delivering consistent, quality work.

Alternatively, if you have the time or budgets are tight, you can roll up your sleeves and dive in. Many owners/managers create a simple schedule and stick to it. They may, for example, handle all outdoor maintenance on Saturdays, and stop by once more per week to clean common areas, pull garbage and recycling and ensure any maintenance issues are resolved. Again, it's entirely up to you.

If you do opt to go it alone, make sure you have a solid on-demand team you can tap into for problems that exceed your abilities. If a pipe bursts in the middle of the night or your basement apartment starts to flood, you need a pro on speed dial—someone who knows the property and can swing into action immediately. Be sure to shore up those professional relationships early on, so you're never left trying to tackle high-level work under pressure.

There are pros and cons to doing the property management yourself:

Pros of In-House Property Management

- You could save money versus hiring a professional engaged 24/7. If you have a few properties in good condition, the extent of your property management could be a lawn mowing, mopping and a sink clog here and there. If you're relatively handy—or are open to learning—managing properties could be a fun new challenge.

- You'll learn the ropes quickly. By getting up-close-and-personal with the day to day operations of your properties, you'll be better equipped to not just transition the work at some point but you'll be better equipped to spot your next great deal.

- Often new investors are shooting in the dark when it comes to what the long-term cash flow will really look like—seasonal changes, marketplace shifts and competition can change your building's occupancy, rental rates and alternative cash flow opportunities. Once you've managed a property or two, you'll start to spot those trends so you can make the most efficient, effective investment decisions down the road. That's incredibly valuable.

- You'll have total control over your properties, without having to work through a manager or management team. While your property manager works for you, they often take control over the day to day operations—you may not even know what's happening behind the scenes. If that's not your style, managing your own properties could be the way to go.

- You care more than anyone when it comes to your investment properties. While the best property managers are, truly, incredible assets, they aren't you. They haven't invested the time, talent and resources to build your portfolio—you have. At the end of the day, no one will ever have the same passion, commitment or care as you do.

Cons of In-House Property Management

- You're flying solo. So that 2:00am pipe burst? You're getting the call and you're getting in the car to handle the issue yourself.

- You'll need to personally handle or oversee everything, from buying garbage bags to calling the tenant about the late rent check. Yes, you can outsource any or all of these tasks, but now you're just managing a team of a people, each with different agendas, different priorities and different levels of consideration for your properties.

- You could end up spending more. With a professional property manager, you know the fee structure going in. If you don't "use" the full breadth of services, you may feel you've overpaid. But if you hit a rough patch, chances are you'll spend more "a-la-carting" it to deal with repairs, emergency work and other issues that may arise. That can be bank-breaking, at best.

Hiring A Professional Property Manager

If your current or near-future cash flow goals exceed the basics—those few single-family homes or a small-scale apartment building, for example—it likely makes sense to hire a professional property manager to oversee all or part of your portfolio.

UNDERSTANDING A PROPERTY MANAGER'S ROLE

Managing an investment property isn't just about basic maintenance and the occasional repair. Managing a property means overseeing *all* aspects of the business, and all aspects of keeping your properties cash flow positive.

Before deciding to manage your own properties yourself—or before underestimating what really goes into a professional property manager's job—consider these tasks. While some are more time-consuming than others, all are required to keep the proverbial trains running. If you hire a property manager to oversee your properties, they'll handle all of it. And if you go it alone? You'll be responsible for everything on this list, including:

- Maintenance, including *general upkeep, tenant maintenance requests, repairs and occasional needs such as painting*

- *Landscaping*, from mowing lawns to trimming shrubs to seasonal plantings, pest issues and more

- Handling *ongoing inspections*, as mandated by your business or your local regulations

- Managing all *taxes and insurance-related needs* for your properties

- Collecting *monthly rent, security deposits, pet deposits and other fees* such as parking and storage. This process involves everything from sending monthly invoices to processing payments to dealing with late payments and penalties.

- *Raising rents* and communicating those changes to tenants

- *Marketing properties/units, ensuring a steady stream of qualified tenants* as units become available

- *Managing all vacancies* as tenants' leases end, evictions happen or, otherwise, units become available

- *Overseeing those evictions*, including notifying tenants and managing the legal side of the process

- *Managing tenant screenings*, including applications, credit checks, collecting deposits, engaging co-signers and executing rental agreements

- *Ensuring all tenants adhere to the lease terms*, and dealing with any violations on a case by case basis

- Managing other aspects of the building experience, including *parking garages, outdoor spaces, shared spaces, laundry rooms, gyms* and more
- *Hiring and managing building staff,* such as doormen, parking attendants, handymen, security and maintenance staff

Handling tenant relations. This includes everything from maintaining positive relationships with new and existing tenants to dealing with complaints, concerns and, overall, making your property a great place to call "home."

When you're striving for scale, you simply don't have the time or resources to properly manage your existing properties. Beyond that, as your business and property count grows, it becomes harder and harder to keep up. For a set fee—usually 4% to 10% of your monthly rental revenue, plus expenses—you can hire a pro.

If you choose the wrong property manager, it can quickly lead to cash flow issues—lack of tenant satisfaction and high turnover, excessive vacancies, poorly maintained properties with sky-high repair costs and other costly challenges that could have been avoided with proper management.

Time and scale aren't the only benefits of using a third-party property manager or management company:

Pros of Hiring a Property Manager

- They have a proper infrastructure and workflows in place, including the right staff, contractors, insurance and screening processes to ensure your properties are managed right—and that your cash flow is always consistent.

- They can handle anything, big or small. Again, if you go it alone, there's likely a limit to your handyman skills—and that could mean big bucks in outside repair costs. Having a property manager ensures you're paying a consistent fee for anything and everything that happens on their watch. For many, that's comforting and cost-effective.

Cons of Hiring a Property Manager

- The costs could outweigh the benefits if your portfolio is small or you aren't generating enough cash flow to pay a property manager. You should be generating meaningful cash flow even with your property manager on the books.

- If not—or if you're losing money on you've added their costs— consider outsourcing a piece of the management responsibilities for now, then revisiting when you have a more substantial monthly income from your properties.

- You'll be spending money even when management costs don't justify it. Chances are, you'll pay your property manager monthly. During that month, they'll carry out a number of services from tenant screenings to rent collecting to general maintenance. Some months, that will be it—and in those months it can feel like you're paying for more than you actually needed.

- You're bringing someone else into your business. While, of course, this isn't a bad thing, you do need to be mindful. Most property managers are good, reliable professionals. Some, though, don't have your best interests at heart—and that can be a problem.

- When you hire anyone—an employee, a vendor, a contractor— you're opening yourself and your business up to their point of view and their processes. This can be a great learning experience, especially when you're new to the industry.

- However, you're also opening yourself up for less-than-ideal hurdles—think fraud, theft and competition. It's not common, but it happens. And when it does, you could be particularly susceptible given the level of trust you've shown and the level of proprietary access they've had.

Choosing The Right Property Manager

If you decide to bring on a third-party, **start by asking for referrals**. In this business, personal referrals are the single best way to find anyone— new hires, property managers, contractors, painters, anyone. If a professional has delivered on their commitment with *other* real estate investors, chances are they'll be reliable and effective for you as well.

Having this vote of confidence from someone you know and trust goes a long way. Not only will you go into the partnership feeling more stable, but you'll cut through the clutter of less-than-ideal candidates, saving you time and headaches. So don't be afraid to ask for referrals—ask fellow real estate investors and landlords you know, start the conversation at local REIA or industry events or post on online or social message boards.

People are always happy to share the good, the bad and the ugly. Take it all in and start your search. If you truly can't find a referral, go online, do a quick search and look at property managers' ratings and reviews. Online reviews have become an incredible resource for everything from where to eat to what to buy to who to hire. Use that to your advantage.

Armed with your initial property manager list, the next step is to **vet them**. Even if you've received dozens of glowing recommendations, it's still important to do your due diligence and personally assess each candidate. Someone might be the *best* property manager on the block, but if they aren't in-step with you, your business and your objectives, it probably doesn't make sense to move forward.

For example, an all-star property manager might have only managed apartment buildings in the past. If you have a portfolio packed with single-family homes or commercial properties, they might not have the insights and immediate intel to get the job done right.

To ensure you ultimately secure the right candidate for the job, be sure to ask these critical questions. Add, adapt or adjust so they're in-sync with your business and your property management needs.

- What are your management fees?
- What is your fee schedule?
- Are there any other costs to consider—one-offs, startup fees, maintenance visit costs, etc.?
- How long have you been a property manager? How long have you been with Company X?
- What properties do you currently manage?
- What types of properties are they?
- Number of units?
- Monthly revenue?
- How many evictions do you deal with in a typical month?
- Average vacancy?
- What is your typical tenant screening process?

- Do you accept tenants with past evictions?

- If so, what are the typical terms?

- How do you handle non-paying tenants?

- How do you market properties/units?

- How do you manage maintenance requests? Can you walk me through a typical request from tenant submission to completion?

One final note: it's important to remember that, even if you do hire a third-party property manager, this should never be an "out of sight, out of mind" experience. Like any partner or vendor, you need to keep tabs on your property manager or management company and ensure they're continuously delivering the quality service, value and efficiency you and your tenants demand.

Even if you've vetted them and even if you've worked with them for *years,* it's essential you never take your eye off the property manager ball. The best property managers can be spread too thin from time to time or get a little too lax with their long-term properties. Look for these and other issues and course-correct early on to ensure your properties are managed properly.

Keeping Property Management In-House

While solo management or hiring a third-party team are common approaches for real estate investors, there is a third option: **keeping property management in-house**. However, keep in mind, you shouldn't choose this option this option initially. You should only hire an in-house part- or full-time property manager when your existing cash flow justifies it.

Alternatively, some real estate investors opt to start their own property management arm of their business. Not only does this enable them to keep their own properties in-house, but it creates a new cash flow stream for the organization—specifically, their property managers can manage *outside* commercial and residential properties, helping add to your monthly revenue.

Done right, it's a win/win—you can keep close tabs on your properties while generating income from your quality property management services. In most cases, you'll want to have thousands of units in your portfolio—5,000 to 10,000, usually—before this makes sense.

While it sounds appealing, it may be best to consider this option 12-24 months from now, if not further down the line. Bringing on employees comes with its own challenges and costs that can make the process even more difficult. Again, it's a good option at some point. For now, focus on the two key avenues at hand: managing your own properties or hiring a third-party property manager.

Your Most Valuable Asset: TIME

There's one final consideration when determining how to handle property management. *Your time.*

Cliché as it may sound, it's true—time is your most valuable asset. You can create more money, invest in more buildings, take more trips, widen your social circle. But you can never make more time. When it's gone, it's gone.

That's why time is so valuable, it's one of our only non-renewing resources. As a real estate investor, you should be investing your time in tasks only you can do—tasks that build your business and create even more cash flow. That could be anything from finding and negotiating new deals to networking at local REIA events to taking a class or attending a seminar on growing your business.

Only you can tackle those tasks and grow your business as a direct result. And *that's* how you should be investing your precious time.

Someone else can clean the tenant's lounge. Someone else can take the recycling to the curb. Someone else can replace light bulbs, mow lawns and unclog sinks.

Only you can increase your cash flow. Keep that in mind as you're determining property management next steps.

CHAPTER 13

ADDING VALUE TO THE PROPERTY

Once investment deals have been done and your properties are being effectively managed, the next step is to think big—as is, how big can you grow the value of this investment property?

"Value add" is a critical piece of the real estate investing puzzle and, done right, can increase your monthly income while lowering your out-of-pocket expenses. Together, that can take a rock solid cash flow property to something even better—something that lends greater value to you and your business every single day.

The idea of "adding value" can apply to many industries and niches. Regardless of the industry, taking steps to add value usually comes down to:

1. Creating more revenue streams or enhancing existing ones, with modest additional investment out of pocket.

2. Driving down operational expenses—in other words, spending less while still generating the same profits.

In most cases, business owners and real estate investors try to do both, driving even greater value add. Think about it. If you were to decrease the amount you spend running your building and increase the amount you're bringing in each month, you'd be in a great position. You would be generating more revenue for less—that means bigger profit margins and a bigger payday for you.

Stabilizing Your Investment Properties

Ultimately, stability is always a goal when you add a new cash flow building into the mix. You want to stabilize your asset—to maximize the value of that property by:

- Fully leasing the building.

- Charging and receiving rents at or above market rates.

- Minimizing tenant turnover and ensuring it's staggered throughout the year—and that you have tenants lined up to slide right in to fill any vacancies.

- Maintaining operating standards with little to no capital improvements.

Some investment properties will be stable when you take them over—they'll be well-maintained, well-functioning and filled with responsible, market rate-paying tenants. But others won't. Other investment buildings will require you to move from unstable—occupancy issues, low rents, major turnover and costly renovations—to stable. These properties are often appealing to investors because they're well-priced—below market value, in many cases. However, the money you save scooping up these properties will likely be reallocated to stabilizing that property in the short-term.

No matter how you achieve stability in your investment properties, the benefits are clear—you'll have less risk and less uncertainty in your portfolio and your monthly cash flow. From there, you'll be able to drive greater returns over time, increasing the market value of your property for the long-term.

Getting to the place of stabilization and creating value add can be achieved through a number of simple steps and strategies. Ultimately, value add comes down to two things: increasing cash flow and/or decreasing operating costs.

Value Add #1: Increase Cash Flow

The first option is where new real estate investors focus first: **increasing cash flow** on their investment property. By driving *up* your revenue without increasing your costs—or increasing them minimally—you'll generate greater ROI for your building that, over time, has the potential to increase even more.

It's a simple concept. For example, if you have a 24-unit building that rents 800-square foot one-bedrooms for $1,200 per unit, you're generating $28,800 per month in rent, less expenses. Anything that increases your income above that $28,800 is added revenue. In this business, that's the name of the game. The good news? There are lots of ways to achieve these increases, any or all of which can be applied to your investment properties.

#1. Make property improvements

A distressed apartment building or commercial center likely won't command the same rents as a high-end luxury property. Investing in the interior and exterior of your building can drive market value up—and, with it, rents. The next time a renovated unit or space is vacant, you can increase the rent. Eventually, your entire space will be renovated and ready to command higher monthly revenue.

#2. Increase rents

If your building is renting below market value—no matter the condition—you can increase rents. Do your due diligence and pull comps like you did when you were initially investigating the property. What are other similar properties renting for? What does their occupancy look like? What is the high and low end of the rent rate spectrum?

As you're looking at comps, be sure you're evaluating properties similar to yours. Ideally, that means rental properties within a ½ -1-mile radius of yours, that sync in terms of square footage, transportation access, parking and other amenities. If you're comparing apartment rentals, be sure you're comparing homes with the same number of bathrooms and bedrooms.

Armed with your comps, you'll see where your buildings fall and be able to determine if it's time to increase rents. For example, let's say you have three comps for your apartment building:

BUILDING 1: 1-bedroom, 880 square feet: $1,550/month
BUILDING 2: 1-bedroom, 905 square feet: $1,710/month
BUILDING 3: 1-bedroom, 790 square feet: $1,300/month

Add up the total monthly rents and divide by the total square footage.

$4,560 total monthly rents / 2,575 square feet = $1.77/square foot

Then, multiple that average amount per square foot by your apartment square footage:

$1.77 x 800 = $1,416

In this case, based on the average monthly rents your comps are commanding, you should be renting your property for $1,416 per month. Increasing your rents at once or over time would drive value add—you'd be making more per unit each month, without spending anything. And because this increase would be market-driven, your building will remain competitive with others in your immediate community. So, once you've done the math, determine if you want to issue blanket rent increases at the end of every lease or increase rates for new tenants as they come in.

#3. Add a way to drive revenue into the mix

There are options for increasing cash flow streams without adding expenses. For example, if you own an apartment building, you could add a laundry room with paid washers and dryers. You could also allocate a portion of your maintenance or storage space for tenant storage, and rent units in different sizes and configurations. Bike parking is another easy add-on—for a set monthly fee, tenants could safely park their bikes in a secure location on-site.

For higher-end buildings, optional add-ons like gyms and fitness centers, concierge services and business centers can also create added revenue streams. Even adding a simple $25 to $50 per year pet fee could increase your revenue.

Commercial buildings also have options. If your building is near public transportation, consider renting parking spaces in your existing lot. Other investors alter their property's intended usage, or divide units. Chances are, two 1,500-square foot storefronts will rent for more than a single 3,000-square foot shop.

#3. Going above and beyond

Beyond building improvements and renovating apartments, consider unit-by-unit opportunities. For example, adding a washer and dryer to a unit could drive monthly rents up for that unit versus a non-washer/dryer unit. Balconies and energy efficient appliances are also options that can add value to individual units. Allocating set parking spots to certain office or commercial space or free Wi-Fi could be good additions as well.

#4. Renegotiate leases

While you want to keep rents at market-rate, having a building filled with stable, steady, rent-paying tenants is a tremendous value to your investment. Consider renegotiating long-term leases with existing tenants, trading those lengthier terms for more modest increases every year or two.

CASE STUDY:

DRIVING VALUE-ADD BY INCREASING CASH FLOW

HURON ESTATES MHP
Cheboygan, MI | Off-Market Acquisition | July 2018

Overview

Huron Estates MHP is an all-ages, affordable community consisting of 111 spaces immediately juxtaposed to the local Wal-Mart. The community was acquired in an off-market, deed-in-lieu of foreclosure transaction.

About the Project

Sunrise received a tip from a podcast listener about a community bank that was interested in selling a non-performing MHP note. In order to take title to the property, we purchased the distressed note from the bank, inserted a court-appointed receiver, performed a deed-in-lieu on the note holder, and took ownership at a deep discount to market value.

The Challenge

Huron Estates experienced years of mismanagement and needed attentive care. A friendly community with fairly modern infrastructure and municipal utilities, the asset had good bones. But the former owner ran the property into the ground, operating at a 74% expense ratio. Massive water leaks went months without attention, landscaping was unkempt, and potholes littered the pavement.

What We Did

Sunrise purchased the note for less than $1mm and began renovations by trimming overgrown trees, planting fresh landscaping, repairing damaged roads, rectifying deferred maintenance, replacing on-site management, stabilizing poor collections, and installing water meters to promote conservation. After significantly improving the community, Sunrise began billing residents for their individual water usage and moved lot rents to just below the market rate.

The Outcome

Sunrise increased the NOI, boosting revenue and lowering the expense ratio to 48%. Within three years, the property value increased by 126%. Having created significant sweat equity, Sunrise decided to sell the asset for $2.25mm, providing investors with an exceptional risk-adjusted return.

Value Add #2: Decrease Operational Expenses

While it may feel impossible, there are ways to decrease your monthly expenses. By reducing expenses that don't impact your revenue, you'll immediately recognize greater ROI for your investment property.

Keep in mind, decreasing operational expenses doesn't necessarily mean giving up amenities or basic comforts. In many cases, it's simply about identifying and acting on efficiencies or finding lower-cost providers and options. It's possible, then, to cut costs without giving anything up—or, depending on your options, vendors and negotiating skills, *gaining* some perks. Some places to start looking:

#1. Monthly bills

Often, investors and property owners are paying for services they don't want, need or even *realize* they're paying for. Look for old accounts you're still paying fees on, optional add-ons to cable and Internet bills and other monthly expenses you mindlessly pay. Do you need them *all?* Or are you paying for *more* than your building actually uses? This is a good place to start because, often, you can cut a few things here and there that weren't being used in the first place.

#2. Consider efficiency

Energy efficient light bulbs are a simple way to save big. Depending on the types of light bulbs you're using now, a single energy efficient light bulb could save you $10 per year. If you have 500 lights in your building, that could translate to $5,000 in savings per year—more for bigger buildings.

If you cover tenants heating bills, another way to reduce your costs could be checking insulation and windows. Without proper insulation and window sealing, it's easy to lose a tremendous amount of heat—and that could result in your tenants turning up the thermostat even more. For each degree your thermostats are down in the winter, you'll save about 3% on your heating bill.

#3. Take down property taxes and insurance

Often, property owners simply go along with property taxes. Over time, though, these can add up.

It's a good idea to have a real estate attorney review your property taxes before close. If they feel they're high, you may be able to appeal or grieve your taxes, lessening your appraisal and, with it, your annual tax bill. Depending on when taxes were last assessed, you could save thousands, month-to-month.

The same goes for your insurance policy. Take some time to review and determine if you have the right coverage—or, even, if you have *too much.* In many cases, simply combining policies under one umbrella or shopping around for other providers can generate significant, ongoing savings. We recently reviewed our policies that easily cut 10% off of our insurance expense without sacrificing any coverage.

#4. Look at management expenses

Whether it's looking at your property manager's agreement and shopping around for other options, re-evaluating maintenance staff or taking over certain day-to-day tasks, there could be some easy ways to reduce management costs.

ADDING VALUE BY SOLVING TENANT ISSUES

We recently invested in a mobile park home in Richmond. It was in great condition, and had little to no deferred maintenance. Gross revenue was well over $240,000 annually.

When we looked at the profit and loss statement and the previous NOI, it was around $28,000—in other words, they had over $200,000 in expenses. We dug deeper and discovered they had a tremendous amount allocated to payroll. From our estimates, one person should have been managing the park— they had four.

Despite having so many managers in place, the mobile home park had *no* tenant screening process. If you had money in hand, you could rent from them. That was a problem. After each tenant left, they invested thousands in getting the space back to new. A new, unscreened tenant would move in and, within months, stop paying. As soon as the eviction process started, the tenant would inevitably trash the place—and the cycle (and expenses) continued.

As soon as we assumed ownership, we cut the staff back to one and implemented a tenant screening process. No longer would we accept felons or people with a history of evictions. Within 12 months, the NOI was $165,000—nearly six times higher with these two simple changes.

CASE STUDY:

DRIVING VALUE ADD BY REDUCING OPERATIONAL COSTS

SHADY GROVE MOBILE HOME PARK
Petersburg, VA | Off-Market Acquisition | Nov 2015

Overview

Shady Grove Mobile Home Park is an all-ages, affordable community consisting of 52 spaces. The community was acquired in an off-market transaction, and sourced via direct-to-owner marketing.

About the Project

Shady Grove Mobile Home Park was identified through our internal marketing efforts. Roughly 80% of our historical transactions have been sourced in this manner. Upon receiving a direct mail piece, the owner contacted our team and was immediately interested in selling the property.

The Challenge

When Sunrise took over the property, the park had $221,000 in Revenue but a mere $27,000 NOI, which depicts major operational inefficiencies. The owner was retired, lived out of state, and preferred not to engage in property management.

What We Did

Sunrise negotiated a $650,000 purchase price, and the previous owner carried financing with the following terms: 25% down payment, 7% interest, with 25-year amortization. We felt confident in our ability to increase NOI to $120,000 shortly after acquisition by instituting more professional property management. Upon acquisition, we put proper leasing practices in place, instituted a large scale marketing effort, scrutinized repair & maintenance, cut payroll, and trimmed unnecessary expenses.

The Outcome

Sunrise increased NOI to $162,000 by increasing revenue and cutting expenses. Having maximized the value of the asset, we decided to sell the property at market, ultimately disposing of the asset for more than $1.8mm in May 2018.

CHAPTER 14
DETERMINING YOUR EXIT

It may sound completely off-base, even counterintuitive, but before diving into a real estate investing strategy, it's essential to think about how you're getting out of the opportunity first. From there, work backward through everything from how you'll manage the property to the cash flow streams to your capital investment—and, beyond that, how this property will coexist with your other investments.

Keep in mind, this is a conversation you should be having with yourself every single time you consider a new real estate investment. While today you may be looking for one-off single-family properties to slowly build your portfolio, a year from now you may be ready for something bigger—and, in five years, something even bigger still.

By continuously reevaluating, you'll give yourself the opportunity to gut-check and determine what makes sense *right now,* pivoting and adjusting to meet your real-time needs.

Strategy #1: Growing your capital over time

Many real estate investors opt to grow their capital investment over time. If, for example, you fixed and flipped your first property while still working full-time, you may have opted to take the revenue and invest it into a larger project. This would enable you to both avoid capital gains tax *and* keep your investing business moving ahead.

As long as you're working or otherwise generating income, this reinvestment process could go on for a while—fixing and flipping properties and pouring *those* funds into your next great investment deals. Eventually, though, if your goal is to replace your full-time income, you'll have to pump the brakes on this cycle. Eventually, you'll need to start taking some of that money as *your* payday.

If that doesn't happen for a few years, it's possible you could have rolled up hundreds of thousands or even *millions* in capital gains. Let's say it's $2 million—that could easily be put towards a $6 million or $7 million investment property which, in turn, could generate enough revenue to replace your 9-to-5.

Strategy #2: Building—and holding—long-term cash flow assets

At the moment, this is my preferred strategy: buying long-term cash flow assets, making improvements, refinancing and holding onto them. This strategy allows us to have passive income from other investments we've built up over time. This has also given us the liquidity to put capital into current and future investments and increase our monthly cash flow considerably.

This is a great approach right now because we no longer have to re-trade every few months or years just so we can enhance our portfolio.

Granted, getting to this strategy may take some time. If you have capital to invest now—cash on hand, money tucked away in self-directed retirement accounts or, even, a partner who can put up cash for your initial investments—you may be able to start here. If not, consider starting with strategy #1 and working your way to #2.

Here's a case study where I implemented the buy, improve, refinance and hold strategy:

CASE STUDY:
BUY, IMPROVE, REFINANCE & HOLD STRATEGY

CEDARHURST & WALSTON MHP
Salisbury, MD | Off-Market Acquisition | Oct 2017

Overview

Cedarhurst & Walston MHPs are all ages, affordable communities totaling 180 spaces along Maryland's Eastern Shore. Both communities were acquired from long-time, legacy owners who developed the properties decades earlier and had kept lot rents at $250 for years, despite the fact that market rates were north of $400.

About the Project

Cedarhurst & Walston MHP were acquired through a pocket listing with a local broker. We'd been in contact with the owners for years but the family wanted to sell the asset via broker, so we nagged (politely) the broker for many months prior to the asset being listed to ensure we would be the preferred buyer.

The Challenge

Over time, the owners had become tired. When Sunrise took over management, abandoned homes were scattered throughout the community and the underground infrastructure was a mess. Both well and septic systems had deferred maintenance. Worse yet, abandoned homes attracted unruly residents and crime to the neighborhood. The poorly managed assets were also in need of general cleanup.

What We Did

Sunrise negotiated a combined $2.6mm purchase price for the properties. Upon acquisition, Sunrise replaced on-site management, pumped septic tanks, demolished unsalvageable abandoned homes, renovated salvageable park-owned-homes, and power washed units. Once aesthetics improved, Sunrise set about recapturing the loss-to-lease.

The Outcome

Sunrise grew the NOI substantially, ultimately increasing lot rents to just beneath the market rate. In June 2019, Sunrise executed a cash-out refinance on the property, returning all investor capital in the process. Investors now have an infinite cash-on-cash return while retaining equity in an asset that appraised for more than $6mm. All told, Sunrise created over $3.5mm in sweat equity within two years on an original investment of $1.1mm.

Determining Your Involvement In Cash Flow Properties

Another key consideration is how involved—or uninvolved—you want to be in your cash flow properties. There's no right or wrong here but, in many ways, where you land will determine the types of investment properties that make sense for you and your business, at least right now. Your feelings will also dictate how big you can grow your portfolio over time—too much involvement could, potentially, cap your growth.

With that said, I don't personally manage my properties. We have a property management company and in-house asset managers who oversee the on-site property management teams. In the beginning, though, I did have a more active role in day-to-day management. My goal was to get to a point where I no longer needed to be so involved. I knew outsourcing all aspects of property management would give me the time I needed to grow my portfolio and my business.

Handing off management to a third party may not be an option from day one. Again, it's all about strategy—about determining your goals and what you want for yourself and your business, then mapping out a path to get there.

For me, it was not managing my properties, and I kept my eyes on that prize until I crossed the finish line with the resources, funds and know-how to turn things over. From there, my investing business took off. I suddenly had the time to seek out new investment deals and drive them to close. I suddenly had resources at my disposal to ensure new properties were well integrated into the business and moving towards stabilization and greater value add. I could focus on scale. I could focus on brand awareness. I could focus on the things only I could do, without worrying about tenant complaints or minor maintenance issues popping up left and right.

While these tasks—the basic maintenance, collecting rent, screening tenants—may seem like quick-hit projects, together they can completely derail your day and, ultimately, your business. Think about it: it may take 30 minutes to screen a tenant, but if you have two people applying that becomes an hour-long commitment. If you have six open units, you're now looking at six hours just to screen tenants. Layer in the calls, the maintenance requests and the basic day-to-day needs that come with managing a building, and it's easy to see how your weeks could be completely absorbed—and how you would hit a ceiling pretty quickly.

Understanding the Exit

It's essential to think about your exit before diving into any new investment deals. This may sound counterintuitive, but it makes sense. Going in, you should know you have a solid, stable plan A, B and C— that even if your primary revenue-driving approach doesn't pan out, you have other approaches to test and fall back on.

We recently bought a mobile home park in Georgia. When we closed, the park was in very rough shape—so rough, I normally wouldn't have pursued it. But, given the price, we had nothing to lose. So we moved ahead with a clear exit strategy—buy the park, renovate it and stabilize the investment so we could drive meaningful, market-level cash flow.

We also had a plan B. If we could get the property where it needed to be, we'd flip it post-renovation. We knew there were plenty of cash buyers out there who would be happy to scoop up this mobile home park, and who could take it to the finish line if we couldn't or wouldn't.

We also had a third option—a plan C if we couldn't move forward with the investment. If we got into the property and, on closer examination, saw it was much more of a time, resource and capital commitment than we'd intended, we'd pump the brakes and wholesale the investment. This would enable us to make a quick buck without the heavy lifting. It wouldn't be ideal, but it wouldn't be the worst thing in the world. If we resorted to plan C, we would generate some revenue with very little effort invested.

Going into the deal with three potential exit strategies gave us a true position of power. We were going to make money on this deal *no matter what.* Once we got in and started working, things definitely didn't progress as we'd hoped, in that "plan A" sort of way. Finding the right teams took longer than anticipated and, when we started bringing in new tenants, it was clear this wasn't the demographic we'd intended— they weren't particularly stable, nor were they qualified to take on this kind of expense.

About 12 months in, we saw it was time to shift our focus to plan B. While we could have generated cash flow from this mobile park, it wasn't worth the time, talent and resources needed to keep it afloat. So, we got the park to 80% stabilization, and found a cash buyer who was eager to take things even further than we had. They were fine dealing with more challenging tenants, and were perfectly comfortable dealing with the ins and outs of this unique mobile home community.

Considering Interest Rates

It's important to have multiple paths to success given the recent market shifts. Interest rates have been record-lows for years, which has driven prices up and made people looser with investment criteria. With so many people racing to pour their money into real estate investments, many are overpaying.

Lenders are working hard to keep pace, stretching their loans to the limits. Whereas a few years ago, you may have seen and been excited about a 70% LTV on a property. But now, it's not uncommon to see 80% or even 85% for a multi-family property.

Think about the implications here. If you have 5-year notes or 5-year balloon loans in place and those properties didn't perform as planned, you could wind up in a situation where your rate is 5% and, in five years, you need to refinance, and now rates are closer to 7%. It's a big difference—and not unheard of.

As interest rates go up, property cap rates usually do as well and, with that, properties lose their value. In that case, you need a plan B. What happens if, in five years, you can't get the right kind of refinancing? What if there's no debt available or the debt coverage ratio isn't enough to get you qualified—at least without putting down your own capital?

When that happens, you need a plan B and a plan C. Too many people are buying blind, and that's a problem. Too often, people scoop up property after property but don't understand the underlying fundamentals of the deal or what could happen if things don't go as planned.

Don't put yourself in that position. Have plans in place so one deal can't derail your business. Inevitably, things will happen and go wrong. If you're prepared, you can pivot and course correct without missing a beat. That's powerful—and that keeps businesses moving forward.

SECTION III

TOP 5 PROFITABLE ASSET CLASSES

In this section, I've included valuable information on my top favorite *5 Most Profitable Asset Classes* to invest in. You'll read about my absolute favorite: mobile home parks (of course!), multi-family properties, self-storage facilities, assisted living facilities and parking lots. I've asked a few of the best and brightest investors—who are experts in their individual niches—to contribute and provide the valuable information you see here.

So once you get through the first sections in this book, I encourage you to thoroughly read on and let these facts sink in as you learn about each asset class and determine which is right for you and your business.

ASSET CLASS #1
MOBILE HOME PARKS
The market has a need. If you can fill it, you can profit.

Our country has a massive affordable housing dilemma. The craziest part? Everyone talks about it, but no one does a thing to resolve it.

That's where you can come in.

We don't—and likely won't—have enough affordable housing to serve the population who needs and wants these properties. Mobile home properties are uniquely positioned to fill this void. But, for a variety of reasons, the market keeps losing mobile home parks. And, each time they do, the need gets greater and the demand skyrockets.

Here's the reality: no matter where you live, no matter where you invest and no matter where you look to build your real estate investing empire, there IS a need for affordable housing—and that means there's a need for mobile home parks.

Too often, developers and investors assume apartment buildings fill that void. However, in my experience, that's far from true. Look at any B or C class apartment complex *anywhere* in the country. Chances are, lot rent in a mobile home park is half *or less* in that same community. And for that significantly lower rent, people can own a home—remember, people *own* the trailer or mobile home and *lease* the land it sits on—and truly invest in their community.

That's important—mobile home parks are true investments and, done right, your tenants will feel and *act* the same. Often mobile home parks come with a stigma. But there's no reason a community needs to be subpar—the mobile home parks we own are incredible communities that my family and I have spent significant time in. There are, without a doubt, some gorgeous mobile home parks out there—stunning communities that go for a fraction of a rundown apartment complex in the same area.

WHAT YOU NEED TO KNOW ABOUT TENANTS

One of the biggest misconceptions about mobile home parks is that the tenants aren't high-quality. I'll cut right to the chase and say that's *not* a universal truth—far from it. And if your tenants *aren't* the most desirable mix, that's on *you*.

First, plan to buy in better neighborhoods—don't park your funds in a community you wouldn't set foot in. They exist, unfortunately, and they're a tough investment to turn around. Aim for working class neighborhoods with blue collar families looking for affordable housing. In other words, look for true middle America. That's a very safe, very smart community to invest in.

Another safe spot? Retirement communities. Many of the better maintained, higher-end mobile home parks are in 55-plus communities. In these instances, retirees move here to have a communal living experience where everything— pools, fitness centers, friends—are within walking or scooting distance. These communities are also appealing because, often, retirees are on a fixed income and want or need to downsize— mobile homes fit the bill.

Once you've invested, ensuring a solid population comes down to who you rent to. Screening tenants for a mobile home park should be like screening tenants for any single-family home. If you wouldn't rent a single-family home to someone based on their credit history, past tenant history, work status or other factors, then don't rent a mobile home lot to them—period. This will preserve the integrity and quality of your community, now and in the future.

In the case of my mobile home park communities, we have solid standards. We screen heavily and don't take felons, sex offenders, people with bad credit or people who don't pay their bills on time. On average, our lots rent for about $300 per month—if the applicant can't afford that, we also pass. If you have a prospective tenant who can't spend $300 per month on rent, there's *nowhere* they can live, short of a friend's couch.

The Benefits Of Investing In Mobile Home Parks

There was a period when I invested in mobile home parks, single-family homes and apartment buildings, plus a little commercial real estate thrown in for good measure. So, for me, it wasn't a "transition." I was always doing a little bit of everything but, still, felt like there were bigger opportunities I wasn't tapping into.

When I couldn't shake that feeling, I moved over 100% to commercial investing—some multi-family, some office buildings, some self-storage and a number of other types of properties. Really, I was just testing out asset classes, assuming that, at some point, I'd stumble on my niche— the path that would help me realize my and my business' full potential and that, ultimately, would "feel" right.

That "right" feeling happened when I went all in on mobile home parks. I've always loved the scalability aspect of multi-family—with one purchase you get multiple units and multiple revenue streams. Mobile home parks, though, took that to the next level. Side-by-side with single-family properties, mobile home park investing just makes sense—here's why.

#1. You're gaining economies of scale

As a mobile home park investor, you're investing in single-family homes without the traditional inefficiencies of single-family homes. On one common piece of ground, an investor could scoop up hundreds of single-family properties, sometimes across multiple neighborhoods or communities.

#2. You're getting better financing

Mobile home parks—and multi-family properties, in general—are easier to finance than multiple single-family homes, *and* there's better financing terms available. It's a more scalable business—the amount of time and effort it takes to build a portfolio of 100 single-family homes one-by-one versus 100 single-family homes in a mobile home park is, simply, incomparable.

#3. You're investing less time and effort managing properties

Managing one-off single-family homes is tricky. Unless you can, somehow, lock in an entire cul-de-sac, you're likely consistently jumping from property to property to property. Keep everything together under one roof or on one common piece of land and inefficiencies go out the window. Everything is *right there* so there's no prioritizing where to focus first or last. Tackling anything from repairs and maintenance to walk-throughs and other asks is consolidated.

Also, most mobile home parks are fairly new. There was a big boom in the 1950s but, after that, most parks were developed in the last 20 to 30 years—relatively new, by real estate standards. As a result, you'll likely have fewer major repairs or maintenance issues to deal with.

#4. You're buying into an asset class with a diminishing supply

There are about 50,000 mobile home parks in the U.S., and every year more and more communities are shut down for redevelopment or because poor management ran them into the ground. Ultimately, more mobile home park communities are shut down than built. From 2007-2016, only 97 new mobile home parks were constructed *nationwide*. That's staggering!

This creates incredible opportunities for investors. There is a diminishing supply of mobile home parks, but there's *always* a demand for affordable, high-quality housing. If you can find a great mobile home park in a good market with solid housing needs, you're in business—literally.

#5. You'll have little to no competition for tenants

Once you *do* invest in a mobile home park, you'll have little to no tenant competition. In this business, there's *rarely* a moment when a

THE CASH FLOW INVESTOR

new developer comes in, buys a plot of land down the road and builds a new mobile home community.

As a real estate investor, that's a huge benefit. You won't wind up dealing with oversupply in this niche, which is a constant threat in any other type of real estate investing. Developers want to put up apartment buildings on the outskirts of town, where mobile home parks usually go—and those really *aren't* a threat. In many of the communities in which we operate, there are tons of apartment complexes right around the corner, but we're still generating tons of buzz and tons of interest every time homes become available.

#6. You'll realize above average returns

Compared to single-family *and* multi-family *and* many types of commercial real estate, mobile home parks have historically generated significantly higher returns. This is true across virtually every market in the U.S. If you can lock down and effectively manage a mobile home park, you'll generate solid returns, now and in the future.

#7. You won't have to deal with turnover

Not only do mobile home parks drive solid ROI, but they tend to have much lower turnover than other real estate investments. In mobile communities, residents own their homes or trailers, and they rent the land or lot from you.

Even though they're called "mobile" homes, they aren't like cars or trucks—it takes *a lot of effort* to move a mobile home, and costs quite a bit as well. Chances are, once a mobile home owner parks on your lot, they're there for the long haul. This compares favorably to a normal apartment building that's turning people over every 12 to 24 months. In fact, the most tenured resident we have has paid lot rent in the community for over 40 years!

#8. You'll have more conscientious homeowners who are invested in YOUR property

Because you're dealing with owners, you'll be dealing with people who *care* about their home and their investment—and that means less work and less worry for you. The majority of mobile home owners plant flowers, landscape around their homes and, overall, take pride in the community—that's not always common with traditional renters.

This will help you maintain your investment in the long-term. You'll still have the average repairs and wear and tear, but will likely spend less time and fewer resources keeping your community safe, clean and functional.

CASE STUDY:
MHP Off-Market Acquisition

GREEN LEVEL MHP
Burlington, NC | Off-Market Acquisition | Nov 2014

Overview

Green Level Mobile Home Park is an all-ages, affordable community consisting of 131 spaces located in the fantastic Raleigh-Durham MSA. The community was acquired in a direct-to-owner, off-market transaction.

About the Project

Green Level MHP was identified through our internal marketing efforts. Our acquisition team makes several thousand cold calls each and every week to create consistent off-market deal flow. Green Level was sourced via cold call, and our lead principal Kevin Bupp began negotiations to purchase the property in a direct-to-owner transaction.

The Challenge

When Sunrise took over the property, the park had numerous infrastructure problems, inferior on-site management, below market rents and poor collections. The original developer held the park for decades before turning management over to his daughter, who was neither maintaining the community properly nor maximizing the value of the asset.

What We Did

Sunrise negotiated a $1,070,000 purchase price, and the previous owner carried financing with the following terms: 10% down payment, 5% interest, with 30-year amortization. Upon acquisition, Sunrise replaced on-site management, power-washed all mobile homes, repaired numerous water leaks, sold all park-owned-home units, and recaptured the loss-to-lease.

The Outcome

Sunrise doubled the property's NOI within the first three years of ownership and returned all investor capital along the way. Investors now have an infinite cash-on-cash return while retaining equity in an asset currently valued at more than $3.5mm. This is how you generate cash flow & build legacy wealth.

MULTI-FAMILY INVESTING WITH ROD KHLEIF

Everybody's got to live somewhere, right? House hacking satisfies that basic human need in one of the smartest ways possible.

Driving Meaningful Wealth With Multi-family Buildings

Rod Khleif knows real estate investing—specifically, driving *serious* wealth by investing in multi-family and apartment buildings. He's personally owned and managed more than 2,000 homes and apartments in his career—and that's just the beginning. In all, Rod's launched dozens of unique businesses over the last four decades, generating tens of millions of dollars in the process.

In addition to his own real estate investing, Rod is highly focused on sharing his insights, intel and personal strategies with other investors. His podcast, *Lifetime Cash Flow Through Real Estate Investing,* has featured many high-profile industry guests, including Dean Graziosi (*Millionaire Success Habits*), Jairek Robbins (high-performance coach), Tom Hopkins (*How to Master the Art of Selling Anything*) and Frank McKinsey (*Make it Big!*).

Lifetime Cash Flow has been downloaded more than 3,000,000 times in the last 18 months alone, making it the number one Real Estate, Business and Education podcast on iTunes. Considering the number of podcasts in that category, that is a tremendous achievement, and it's one that's enabled Rod to impact *millions* of real estate investors and entrepreneurs with his powerful message and actionable strategies.

Building a Portfolio One Unit at a Time

Rod's go-to investing strategy is anchored in multi-family buildings, including apartment buildings. For Rod, the benefit is clear: one transaction driving *multiple* income-producing units. It's one negotiation, one loan, one inspection and one location. With that, you'll get five, 10, 15, 20 even 100 units, all generating revenue. Think about what it would take to achieve that by investing in one-off single-family properties. It's an economy of scale play that helps bring down the per-unit acquisition cost versus single-family property investing. When you're considering cash-on-cash, that lower cost is a major win.

Besides scale, with multi-family, you aren't reliant on *one* investment property. If you have 20 units in a single property and *one* is vacant, you still make money on the other 19. If you have *one* single-family property and it's vacant, you make *no* money.

Some other benefits are:

- It's *true* passive investing—get paid even while on vacation.

- It's not as time consuming because the properties are all in one location.

- Cash flow is stable—during the Recession my portfolio took a hit, *except* my apartment buildings.

- It's easy to increase value because value is based on *income,* not value like single-family homes.

- There are *tons* of tax breaks for people who invest in multifamily properties.

And besides that, you're providing an amazing service to people who want, need and deserve affordable, high-quality housing. All of this, and you can easily generate $10,000, $50,000, even $100,000 per month or more.

Financing Multi-family Properties

Multi-family is a win when it comes to financing. As a new investor, you're an unproven entity, but that doesn't mean you can't or won't be funded. By showing you're investing in a property with multiple income streams, you'll definitely drive more interest among banks and lenders. When a lender sees multiple units paying rent each month, they'll feel more confident *you* can keep up with your mortgage even if you wind up with a longer-term vacancy or non-paying tenant.

Lenders also usually "count" 75% of the income from revenue-driving units when considering you for a mortgage. Think about that. Let's say you have a four-unit complex and each rents for $1,500 per month, you'll be generating $4,500 in cash flow every 30 days. That fourth unit is your home.

Of that $4,500, the bank will count about $3,000 of that money as income in *your favor*. That will help you qualify for higher loan limits and give you an overall more robust application going in, even if you're a first-timer. You'll be especially well-positioned with a standard FHA loan. Consider the 2019 limits:

SINGLE FAMILY	
Low-cost markets	$314,827
Standard	$474,350
High-cost markets	$726,525
MULTIFAMILY (standard / high cost)	
Two-unit properties	$403,125 / $903,300
Three-unit properties	$487,250 / $1,124,475
Four-unit homes	$605,525 / $1,397,400

Right out of the gate, you'll be eligible for more financing just because you're coming to the table with a multi-family property. And because you're living in the property, you're getting the added benefit of having your tenants essentially paying for your home, *and* you'll get tons of write-offs because it's your primary residence.

Commercial vs. Residential

The financing piece is a major benefit to investing in multi-family. As Rod explains, commercial real estate investing can seem "scary" right out of the gate, and he's not wrong. With a minor investment of 8-10 hours per week, a new investor can learn the ropes and manage their properties while simultaneously building their portfolio. That's hard to beat. Start with a multi-family and build your courage so you can dive into commercial real estate in a big way.

Building Up and Giving Back

Like me, Rod believes strongly in building your business, building your wealth and giving back as you continue to grow and thrive. In fact, I started our own mobile home park back-to-school backpack brigade after seeing Rod's initiative in action.

As the founder of the Tiny Hands Foundation—a children's charitable organization—Rod rolls out this powerful brigade every fall, providing thousands of filled bags to community schools in need. This foundation is so close to my own heart that I've in turn raised hundreds of thousands of dollars through my own initiatives for his foundation.

He also oversees a Teddy Bear Bridge, gathering bears police officers can use to comfort kids in distress, plus a Holiday Basket Brigade to ensure local families have an amazing holiday. To date, he and his organizations have helped more than 60,000 children in their community—it's impressive and it truly speaks to Rod's character and how he's prioritized giving back, especially in light of his meteoric successes

Getting Started With Rod's Multi-Family Plan

To get started, Rod recommends a 10-step plan. Done right, he explains, this process can drive long-term cash flow through multi-family investing.

#1. Look at your finances

Do a self-evaluation of your current financial state. Do you have money to put down on a property, or will you need a loan or a partner with capital? Looking at your personal credit history and score, will you qualify for a conventional loan? An FHA loan? Are there any quick-hit strategies you can employ to increase your cash on hand, your credit or *both*—for example, paying off a high-interest credit card or moving funds to a self-directed IRA (SDIRA) versus leaving money in a low-yield 401K?

#2. Determine how you want to move forward

While there are countless ways to get started on the multi-family scene, Rod recommends "house hacking" for beginners. The strategy is simple: buy a residential, multi-family property with four units or less—and strong cash flow. Live in one unit and rent out the remaining one to three units. More on this to come.

Of course, this isn't the only option. Most new investors choose a residential 2-4 unit property or small commercial property—an apartment building with 30 units or less, ideally. Depending on your market, your working capital and your goals, one of these options may be a better jumping-off point. Only you can decide.

#3. Determine your market

Choose a market with employment and job growth, income growth, population growth and at least a few major employers. Many people opt to invest in their immediate area—they know and presumably like the area, and have a good sense of where the market is and where it's going. That, though, isn't cast in stone, as Rod explains—there are 2.25 million multi-family properties from coast-to-coast, meaning ample opportunity wherever you look.

#4. Connect with a local agent or broker

This isn't a process you want to tackle solo. Once you've determined the type of multi-family investments you're after *and* the specific market, find a qualified agent or broker in that area who can help drive your search. This person will not only be able to spot deals before they hit the market, but they'll have the inside scoop on everyone and everything—and that's helpful when you start negotiating.

#5. Build investor relationships

No matter your goals and your personal financial situation, it's a good idea to start networking with potential investors in your area. Remember, your relationships should be about more than just real estate. Talk sports, grab dinner, tackle a community service project together—anything that brings you and your potential investing partner together and breaks down potential barriers.

#6. Become a business

Real estate investing isn't a hobby, it's a business, and you need to treat it that way. While there's no need to officially incorporate or spend money creating an LLC, *do* print professional looking business cards, launch a basic website and get a business phone number and sync it to Google Voice.

This should take an hour or two max—and if you aren't super design savvy, grab a freelancer from a site like Fiverr or Upwork. On these sites, you'll find rated and reviewed designers who can get you started for a few bucks.

#7. Build an owner database

If you have existing leads and other contacts, organize them into an owner/seller database—even a simple Excel grid or free CRM will do the trick. If you don't have one, start building one. Literally, everyone you come in contact with via networking or other business outreach goes on your list. If you're still feeling light, consider supplementing with a paid list—many direct mail companies rent or sell targeted lists.

#8. Launch your first direct mail campaign

You'll be working with an agent or broker to find on-the-market and soon-to-be-on-the-market deals. Why not take things a step further and be proactive? Use your list from the prior step and get a direct mail campaign out the door. Even a few letters to the right audience can drive serious results. Rod recently interviewed a new real estate investor in Houston who followed this advice, sent about 300 letters and, from it, wound up landing a 32-unit property that's driving $10,000 in monthly passive income. That's a serious win.

#9. Implement other marketing outreach

Don't forget about other marketing and outreach methods—scouring Craigslist, posting a few ads, Pay Per Click ads on Google or Facebook and advertising in local classifieds and attending auctions, even, can give you a serious leg up and help you better compete with your fellow investors.

#10. Practice analyzing deals

This is critically important to the success of your business, now and in the future. You *must* become an expert at analyzing every deal that crosses your inbox. You need to know that 2-4 family properties are valued based on comps, and anything five-units and up is based on NOI and cap rate.

While it sounds complicated, this step is simple. You need to practice reviewing and analyzing deals daily so you can start analyzing opportunities on the fly.

Housing Hacking 101: What it Looks Like & Why You Want In

So what does house hacking look like? Consider this scenario: You have 5% to put down, so are opting for an FHA loan versus a conventional mortgage. Rod breaks down what the two options look like side-by-side:

SINGLE FAMILY. You find a house you love for $300,000 and can put 5% down on a 30-year loan at 4% interest. Assuming a tax rate of 1.5% and insurance at $2,000 per year, that'd put your monthly payment at about $2,000/month. You might decide to rent out a room or two. If not, that $2,000 is entirely on you.

DUPLEX. Let's imagine you instead choose a duplex at the same price point, down payment, and loan terms. Let's put the rent at $1,250—the national average for a two-bedroom. Congratulations. You've effectively lowered your monthly housing obligation to $750. Not bad.

TRIPLEX. Rod explains that you're in even better cash flow shape. Assuming your rented properties are each two-bedrooms, your monthly gross income will rise to $2,500, giving you a $500 monthly surplus—money you can apply to expenses, capital improvements and other costs to help drive rent *up* in the future.

Soon enough, you'll be able to pocket that money as income and, ideally, it will have gone up with your ongoing reinvestments. The goal? Get you out of the complex and into a single-family home quickly. Not only is that likely where you'd *rather* be, but you'll instantly free up another unit in your building to rent out for even greater cash flow—bonus.

You'll also get another "bonus:" you'll learn to manage a real estate investment. If you've never done this before, living on-property will force your hand and ensure you walk away with the know-how you need to keep investing and, ultimately, manage *others* on the feeding and care of your investment properties.

As soon as you move in, you'll become the onsite supervisor and manager, dealing with everything from burnt-out light bulbs to backed up washing machines to tenant screenings, rent collection, evictions and *everything* in between. Sure, all or most of this will be outsourced, but you'll still be in the middle of all the action, calling the shots.

Rod always reminds new investors that passive income is a goal—a goal that's often years down the road. Don't expect to dive into multi-family or apartment buildings and be an overnight millionaire.

Over time, it happens. You will have high-performing properties that operate like clockwork and deliver revenue month-after-month, as planned. You could be on a beach sipping drinks or shoveling the driveway at your investment property. It doesn't matter whether you are or aren't putting elbow grease into the process—it *will* deliver. But, again, it takes time.

READY TO GET STARTED WITH MULTIFAMILY AND APARTMENT COMPLEX INVESTING?

Download Rod's FREE BOOK, *How to Create Lifetime Cash Flow Through Multifamily Properties.* This free deep dive walks new investors through the entire multi-family investing process, ensuring you can hit the ground running and start driving serious cash flow through multi-family properties. https://rodkhleif.com/books/

SELF-STORAGE WITH SCOTT MYERS

I am not pretending to be something I am not. I am not saying I am better than others who teach people how to invest in self-storage or other forms of real estate. I am not an expert at money or financial success–although I have gone from being bankrupt to being a multi-millionaire.

Driving Serious Cash Flow with Self-Storage

Scott Meyers is a true industry innovator. Long dubbed the nation's leading expert on self-storage, he's taken a niche business and turned it on its head—and he's generated millions in the process.

Scott initially jumped into real estate investing more than 25 years ago. Since then, he's dabbled in a variety of fields before settling on self-storage. His company, Self-Storage Investing, has been involved in over 30 deals, 7,000-plus units spanning 200,000 square feet of self-storage.

His company has 300 equity partners who work with him and his team on these lucrative facilities, and he's identified and raised more $50 million to fund his deals.

Today, Scott continues to invest in self-storage, but focuses a good portion of his time, talent and resources to teaching other real estate investors the rules of the road. The education arm of his business launched in 2007, with a software and learning platform, Self-Storage Profits, Inc. Since then, more than 2,000 student investors have participated in his training programs.

Through his online trainings, live events and masterminds, Scott caters his approach and his message to investors at all levels, from true novices to experienced self-storage owners looking for growth, scale and massive monthly income. His sought-after programs include Complete Guide to Finding and Purchasing Self-Storage Facilities, his Self-Storage Academy live event, Developer's Academy live event, Private Money & Syndication Summit, The Self-Storage Mastermind and his customized mentoring programs.

Building His Business Again and Again

While there's a lot Scott brings to the table in terms of experience and insights, there's another thing I've always deeply respected about him as a real estate investor. Not only is he humble, approachable and committed to helping other investors be successful, he's *very* open about his own path to real estate investing success—a path that wasn't always mistake-free. After 9/11, he lost everything and went from being a millionaire to having his credit card declined over a bag of groceries.

But Scott preserved and rebuilt. And that's what's so impressive, to me. Scott is the real deal. Not only did he build a real estate investing empire once, but he had the strength—and strength of character—to do it again, even better than the first time.

Scott is very transparent—he's the first person to share a deal gone bad or share about his experiences dealing with everything from bankruptcy to problematic investments to dealing with *very* challenging clients and partners. The reality? We *all* deal with challenges in our journeys to success, whether those journeys are in real estate investing or, literally, anything else.

Scott gets it—and he's been there, done that and, now, is better for it. As he often explains, he is who he is because of those mistakes. He's an expert, then, not just in real estate investing, but in *not* making the same mistake twice. And that's made him successful, sought-after and *financially free.*

Why Self-Storage is Thriving—and isn't Slowing Down

While self-storage may seem like a fairly basic, fairly straightforward business, Scott is the first to explain it's anything *but.* Based on his booming business, it's clear self-storage is one of the hottest niches in real estate investing. More people are looking to rent storage units of all shapes, sizes and configurations, creating unparalleled demand in the market. If you have a self-storage facility, you *will* make money, he explains.

And, looking at the market, that success makes sense—and seems pretty clear-cut. According to the *Self-Storage Almanac (SSA),* nearly one in 10 American households rents a self-storage unit. That's a massive percentage of the population—and, each year, the value of those storage units grows.

According to *SSA,* between 2017 and 2018, the monthly fee for a 5' x 10' storage unit increased 5.46%. A 10' x 15' unit average monthly cost increased 9.6% year-over-year—and that's without the owner doing *anything* in terms of value add or renovations. Chances are, those owners spent the same or even *less* to maintain their facility as they did the year prior.

Understanding the Self-Storage Market

So, first, a quick step back to define this unique corner of the market. Self-storage encompasses any storage space—storage rooms, lockers, containers and outdoor spaces—rented to tenants. Contracts tend to be month-to-month and, while most opt for short-term leases, some choose to leave their possessions in storage for months, years or even decades—and when they do, the owner of those units generates revenue.

Depending on the structure of your self-storage facility and units, people and/or businesses may rent out and use the spaces. Larger, warehouse-style self-storage is, often, ideal for companies who need to park equipment, archives and records or other oversized items, while smaller units tend to be scooped up by individuals—people who want to store off-season items, for example, or items they don't need in their typical day-to-day lives.

Most self-storage units tend to range in size from 5' x 5' to about 10' x 30'. If you're considering this space for an individual or household, a 5' x 5' tends to be used for clothing, household items or other smaller pieces—it's about the size of a walk-in closet. On the other end of the spectrum, the 10' x 30' could, likely, fit the contents of an entire *large* house. Other common sizes include:

10' x 10'—fits contents of one larger room, like a living room or family room

10' x 15'—fits two to three bedrooms

10' x 20'—fits multiple rooms or, even, a small to medium house

Though prices vary, the average national storage rates are:

5' x 5': $40 - $50/month

10' x 15': $75 - $140/month

10' x 20': $85 - $155/month

10' x 30': $105 - $190/month

20' x 20': $225/month

Granted, these rates tend to be higher in costlier metro markets and lower in smaller, more rural areas. If your facility offers climate controlled units, assume you can charge a higher rate, 10% to 50% above basic units, if not more.

Think about those numbers, even on a very basic level. If you have a facility with 100 10' x 15' units, 25 5' x 5' units and 25 10' x 30' units, *even on the low end* you could be generating $11,125 per month—that's $133,500 per year.

25   5' x 5' @ $40/month = $1,000/month

25   10' x 30' @ $105/month = $2,625/month

100   10' x 15' @ $75/month = $7,500/month

= $133,500/year

THE CASH FLOW INVESTOR

Regardless of the size, though, self-storage units can *only* be used for storage—people can't live or work in these units, no matter how big. That's a major perk to investing in self-storage facilities. You'll be able to create tremendous wealth *without* having to deal with the hassles of traditional renters.

Yes, you'll have to keep your storage spaces safe, clean, dry and climate-controlled but, beyond that, you're dealing with very little. You'll *never* get a noise complaint from a cranky tenant, or have to worry about heavy duty landscape or maintaining common spaces. Provide a secure spot for people to store important possessions, and you're good to go.

Benefits of Self-Storage Investing

Self-storage is also a great way to diversify your investment risk. Invest in a single-family home and, if you aren't actively renting it to a paying tenant, you're generating *zero* income, but likely still spending money on everything from a mortgage or loan to property taxes, landscaping, marketing and more.

There's also an economy of scale at work every time you invest in self-storage. With one down payment, one loan and one close, you could get 50, 100, 200, even 1,000 or more self-storage units. Think about that for a minute. Buy a single-family home and you're creating one cash flow. Buy a duplex and you're creating two. Invest in a self-storage facility and, suddenly, you have dozens if not hundreds of cash-flow positive units, with rent-paying tenants and tons of opportunity for growth.

Once you're in, self-storage facilities are the epitome of passive income. If you're local, have the time and want to manage your facility, great. If you want to invest and hire someone to manage the day-to-day of your property, also great. Either way, the checks keep coming in month after month—and the monthly revenue is solid. On average, self-storage facilities sell for about $25 to $40 per square foot. Within 12 to 18 months, you could easily pay off your loan—or recoup your capital—and be *very* cash flow positive.

There's a lot of flexibility with this niche. Promotions, for example, can vary from facility to facility depending on your market and what you think your renters want and need. Some self-storage facilities offer free pickups or deliveries, while others have trucks tenants can use to bring items back and forth. Others offer long-term leases with little to no rental increases, or free months early on—others don't.

There are some challenges. The biggest? Turnover. Assume 7% to 8% of tenants will move out each month, giving these investments an added layer of marketing, screening and overall operations. At the same time, though, it's an incredibly safe investment and the asset class with the lowest foreclosure rate. Even during a recession, self-storage tends to perform.

A Father/Son Self-Storage Team Make Their Mark

David Babb is just one of the countless success stories emerging from Scott's training. David and his son Cody attended Self-Storage Academy and, once they finished, the two were completely pumped up about taking their next step into commercial investing.

After doing their due diligence, the father/son pair found and secured a 20,8000-square foot REO in mid-December. The property previously had a $600,000 note, but David and Cody acted quickly and used techniques they'd learned in the Academy to get the deal *done*—by *December 31.*

The bank that had the prior note financed it with a purchase price of $310,000—*after* the bank installed a gate system *at their cost.* David and Cody also asked for six months interest free with *zero* payments. Though the bank declined, they *did* come back with four months of no payments with a 4% rate amortized over 20 years, plus a 10-year balloon. They also received a promissory note for $620,000, which gave them four months to come up with a down payment.

This particular storage facility has 115 units with physical occupancy of 35%. The facility is less than four years old—another win—and has an onsite apartment. In exchange for free rent, they have someone who can manage the day-to-day of the facility, while David and Cody collect their passive income.

Getting Started with Self-Storage

If you decide to get started in self-storage investing, know this: you aren't alone. For nearly two-thirds of self-storage facility owners, this is the *only* commercial property they own. Even if you're a one-off—and even if you're never invested in commercial or in *any* real estate—you're very safe diving into self-storage.

Like any ramp-up, getting started with self-storage means getting your real estate investing house in order. You never want to overpay, so it's essential to know your market or the market you're investing in.

Understand what a "good" deal looks like and what would constitute overpaying. Understand what people are renting—the sizes of units, the terms, the promotions—and who's renting, be it corporate accounts or individuals. And, of course, understand your budget. Do you have money to personally invest? Can you tap into a 401K or self-directed IRA (SDIRA) or a second mortgage to fund your initial investments—or do you have a potential business partner or private money lender who can help you get off the ground?

Once you've established a baseline, *go*. There's never been a better time to invest in self-storage. For years, REITs had been scooping up self-storage facilities in bulk. But, recently, they've stopped, giving one-off and individual investors a solid opportunity to get in on the action without the competition from major REIT investors.

Start your search by looking outside of the traditional REIT circle— ideally, 25,000- to 30,000-square foot properties on enough property that you could easily expand in the future. Alternatively, look for a vacant commercial space and see about repurposing it. It's not hard to restructure a massive warehouse, for example, into 100 storage units— and 100 monthly cash flows.

No matter your approach, Scott advises starting local before expanding. Be on the hunt for storage facilities you can personally manage or, at least, pop in on every now and again. If you're in Maryland and your facility is in Montana, that's a tall order. If, though, you purchase a relatively local facility, you can be front-and-center for all of the major decisions—and, equally importantly, can learn the ropes first-hand so you can make smarter, more strategic investments in the future.

And, according to Scott, you should keep investing in this lucrative niche. Self-storage units are recession-resistant, inflation-resistant and affordable enough that you rarely have to worry about non-paying tenants—or losing your cash flow entirely.

Register for Scott's free self-storage training, How to Achieve Total Self-Storage World Domination *and learn the ins, outs and expert next steps to drive your investing forward. https:// selfstorageinvesting.com/live-events/register-interest/*

ASSET CLASS #4
ASSISTED LIVING WITH GENE GUARINO

Residential Assisted Living Academy has developed and perfected a unique formula that will allow you to take advantage of the massive growth in the senior services market and protect your money while securing your financial future from economic downturns, market crashes and even job losses.

How Gene Guarino Created a Unique Investing Niche

Gene Guarino knows real estate—and, specifically, how to turn a single family home into a monthly cash flow *machine*. His method? Creating and investing in assisted living homes for multiple residents.

For nearly four decades, Gene has been both a business owner and investor, creating his "RAL"—Residential Assisted Living—method, which he teaches around the clock through his RAL Academy. His real estate investing approach is, truly, like nothing I've ever seen before. It's simple even for newcomers, and all but guarantees *serious* success.

Gene's background is truly unique. His mother needed assisted living and he didn't want to put her in a "big box" home. He wanted something more comfortable, more personal and more like *home*—but with the amenities, assistance and support of a traditional community. When he couldn't find what he wanted, he created it, and RAL was born. Now, the company is on a mission to create more than 1,000 homes from coast-to-coast by the end of 2020, and they're well on their way to doing just that.

A Single Family House That Nets Serious Positive Cash Flow

Real estate investing is one of the safest investments out there. The fact is, everyone needs a place to live. If you can provide safe, clean, appropriately-priced housing, you're in business—literally. The same goes for residential assisted living.

As Gene explains, residential assisted living is even *safer*—and more explosive—than traditional real estate investments. Think about the basic dynamics of the aging market. Today, 50% of consumer expenditures are made by seniors, and this growing population controls over 60% of all financial assets in the U.S. That is just the beginning.

In 2015, just over 8% of the population was 65 or older. By 2030, that number is expected to grow to 17%. Americans are living longer, and that means *more* seniors will need *more* places to call "home" in the near future. Again, it comes back to the basic value proposition of real estate investing as a whole—provide the solution and you'll drive cash flow.

It also comes down to the lack of housing for this group. Housing, says Gene, is the number one challenge for the aging population. By investing in assisted living homes, you are providing an incredible solution to a massive problem—and you're generating significant income in the process. Continue to capitalize on this need and this growing population, and your cash flow will only grow—and given this population is showing no signs of slowing down, neither will your monthly income.

Do Good and Do Well with Assisted Living Investments

It's not just the population boom that makes this investing route so lucrative. The average cost for a private room in an assisted living facility is more than $3,750 per month, Gene reports.

But that's not what his approach hinges on. His approach hinges on single-family homes that become assisted living communities—a multi-bedroom home that can house multiple senior citizens, while providing the medical, social and physical support they require. It's a simple approach, even for new investors. You aren't managing hundreds of beds but, instead, a more modest investment property filled with quality, paying tenants.

With that in mind, the economics of it start to really come together—and they're rock solid. A single-family home dedicated to assisted living, for example, can easily net $10,000 per month or more. With one property, you can be set for life. Or, you can keep expanding and growing your empire.

Here, seniors will get "ADLs"—activities of daily living. This isn't a nursing home and this isn't *Golden Girls*. This is something in between. This is residential assisted living, with 24/7 caregivers in a "regular" house with a group of seniors living life *together*. It's doing good *and* doing well. You're doing well by generating a steady monthly income.

And that monthly income is derived from providing a much-needed service in your community. That's powerful.

Now the best part of Gene's approach: you don't manage the property or deal with the tenants. Here's how it works:

- You start an LLC and lease the property *to yourself.*
- You hire a manager and caregiver to manage the tenants and ensure your property is operating like a quality assisted living home.
- Your manager leases out the rooms and deals with day-to-day expenses, tenant needs and other property management to-dos.
- You kick back and cash your checks.

Once in place, your manager and caregivers will also deal with filling the rooms, managing caregivers and providing for those ADLs. All you'll do is lease your investment property to *yourself* and ensure you have the team in place to keep the trains running.

This process is very stable. Most people who own real estate make $100-$200 per month after their expenses—a single vacancy could wipe out a year of passive income. But, in assisted living situations, you're covered. You'll wind up with a long-term tenant with low-impact usage—a group of seniors, managed by a business and strong managers and caregivers. It's an ideal situation that drives significant residual income.

Let's look at the numbers. In this example, let's say you can have 10 seniors living in your property, each paying the U.S. average of $3,750 per month.

$3,750 per month

X 10 beds

= \$37,500 monthly gross income

Of course, you'll also have expenses. If you did *everything* yourself—cooking, laundry, managing tenants, handling ADLs—you'd probably spend about \$10,000 per month on expenses. And many people do. Many people make this their business and handle *everything*.

But that's not Gene's approach. With his method, you'll hire the manager, caregivers and anyone else you need to run your assisted living home. Expenses, in this example, could easily be \$20,000 per month, plus your debt service—that's another \$5,000, he explains.

Even with these seemingly high expenses, though, your profits are still massive. Hire *everyone* and truly invest in a quality assisted living experience, and your expenses on this 10-bed home will be about \$25,000 to \$27,500. But, again, you're pulling in \$37,500 per month—that's \$10,000 in *income* on a single home. And that's more than double the average U.S. household income… on *one property*. Keep going and it's easy to see how your income can skyrocket.

Also, Gene notes, this is the *average*. In many upscale communities and assisted living homes, it's common to generate \$5,000 per bed or more each month, with expenses inching up very little, if at all. Think about that—if you generated \$5,000 per month for those same 10 beds, you'd be generating \$50,000 per month. Even if your expenses went from \$20,000 to \$25,000 and your debt servicing rises by \$2,000, your monthly net income still grows to \$18,000 *per month*. It's staggering.

Next Steps: Getting Started with Assisted Living Communities

For new investors, Gene says, this approach is much easier and much less work than a traditional fix-and-flip—and requires *much* less capital.

There are also, as he notes, *many* ways to get started with assisted living communities.

1. You can OWN the real estate and lease it to an existing assisted living operator for a huge profit—think twice the fair market value, in most cases.

2. You can buy and convert a home for use as a RAL and sell it to a RAL operator.

3. You can own the home *and* own the RAL business.

4. You can do nothing—and, ultimately, you'll likely wind up in an assisted living community, paying $10,000 to $12,000 per month down the road.

The last option isn't *truly* an option—but many people do it. Own your own RAL business—or rent out to an operator—and you're creating consistent cash flow *and* creating a place to live in the future. That's a huge burden off of your family *and* a lasting income stream you and they can count on for the long haul. That's powerful.

So the *real* options. First, you could buy the land and design and build an assisted living home. That's a great option if you have 12-24 months to spare and capital to get the job done. Easier? Buy an existing house and remodel is for your senior tenants. That, typically, takes about 6-12 months and is a much easier approach, especially for new real estate investors. Assume you'll need to tackle a few key renovations such as:

- Adding grab bars to all bathrooms, toilets and showers
- Removing bath tubs and adding roll-in or walk-in showers
- Ensuring there are ramps at entrances and throughout the home

- Widening doors to accommodate wheelchairs, walkers, scooters and aides supporting tenants
- Removing carpets and ensuring smooth surfaces in the home

An even *simpler* approach? Find and buy an existing assisted living home and do a quick rehab. This usually takes 2-6 months and doesn't require the hefty time, talent or cash investment, since the bones are already there.

If you renovate or build a property, you could consider renting out or selling to a RAL—selling this type of home could net you $50,000 to $100,000 or more. If you acquire the license to operate an assisted living business as well, you could be looking at a business worth upwards of $300,000 or more, plus the real estate. Selling it could be a great way to make a (fairly) quick profit.

Alternatively, you can start renting out your *existing* home or be the RAL and investor—those options could have you up and running in 30-60 days. Think about *that* for a minute. In one month from now, you could be running a serious real estate investing business and generating $10,000 or more in *revenue.* It's staggering.

Ideally, as Gene explains, you want to start by being the RAL business *and* the homeowner. A RAL business can generate the big bucks—the $10,000+ per month.

> For more information, check out Gene's training. This comprehensive program will help you generate $10,000, $20,000 or even $30,000 or more per month with assisted living investments. https://residentialassistedlivingacademy.com/ral101/

ASSET CLASS #5
PARKING LOT INVESTING WITH BRIAN SPEAR

Parking lot investments provide clear opportunities for many of today's investors. In the coming 10 or so years, parking lot investments will be a nice addition to any portfolio, though today they tend to be overlooked. Plenty of reasons exist for wanting to invest in parking lots right now.

In order to create legacy wealth, you need to build a portfolio of assets and hold onto them over long periods of time. To that end, we want to focus on niches with favorable long-term economics. This means investing in a niche where the demand grows at a higher rate than the new supply coming online. These favorable long-term economics will serve as a tailwind helping contribute to outsized investment returns over time.

Why Parking – Supply Is Falling

Right now, there are over 40,000 parking lot facilities throughout the U.S., according to the National Parking Association. However, that number isn't growing; it's shrinking. From 2008 through 2017, there's been a 7% drop in the number of facilities across the country.

As the population grows, cities become more dense, and land must be repurposed to fit the needs of the larger population. Parking lots don't generate as much value to the local economy as office space, housing, retail, or entertainment, so there is little incentive to preserve them. Plus, parking lots are one of the easiest types of properties to redevelop. So they are the first option developers look at for new construction opportunities.

There is also political pressure to lower the supply of parking. UCLA professor Donald Shoup has been researching parking for decades. His data reports that too much parking in any city actually hurts the economy by increasing housing costs and puts financial pressure on those who don't own a car. For this reason, several cities have banned the creation of new parking spaces in downtown spaces.

The direct benefit here, then, is that with a limited amount of supply, the value of existing parking lots is driven up, especially for those who invest in this strategy early on.

Demand Is Growing

The demand for parking is massive and continues to increase. Parking demand is a function of population growth and transportation habits. And as everybody knows, the population has historically increased and is expected to increase precipitously over the next several decades, from 329 million today to over 450 million by 2050. As those high-rise complexes go up in downtown areas, the population density grows. When Millennials and Gen-Z establish households, they need somewhere to park their vehicles. So the demand for available parking is driven up.

The number of cars on the road is increasing, too. Estimates are that as of 2022, there are 289 million vehicles on American roadways. That number is expected to climb to over 350 million vehicles within the next 20 years. Consumers have a relatively constant need for their vehicles. That means there is nearly always a demand for parking services in some form. There's no doubt parking will continue to be in demand for years to come, even as there is a shift towards walkable business districts. People have to park their cars somewhere!

The Opportunity Is Rich

Another key benefit to parking lot investments is the current ownership of existing lots. Many are mom-and-pop owners, individuals who are still taking just cash for their lot fees. Several work as their own attendants, too, with few, if any employees. If they do have staff, they trust these individuals with the cash they are given, operating a very simple system. Many are not interested in improving lots or their business's functions.

This creates a clear and even simplistic opportunity for investors to improve the business model. Investors can employ improved technology, operational efficiency and profit-boosting techniques to drive up what the average lot earns. For those looking for a nice margin of safety in their investment, parking lot properties can often provide it.

Income Is Steady and Recurring

Unlike other property investment strategies, parking lot investments provide a very stable earning strategy. There are two options:

1. **Operate Yourself:** In this model, you'll manage the operations yourself. With the right technology and upgrades, it can require little actual in-person management.

2. **Third-Party Operators:** A sometimes better option is to leverage third-party operators. For a set amount of money a month on a five- or ten-year lease, third party operators can manage the property for you. You can incorporate rent increases tied to inflation. Using a third-party operator can be ideal for those who want less of a hands-on operation but predictable cash flow.

Investing with Less Competition Means Better Strategies

Another key aspect to keep in mind is the actual amount of competition in this asset class. Parking is nearly always overlooked when considering asset classes. That's a good thing for investors because it means there's far fewer competitors working against you. In this fragmented marketplace, there's more opportunity to buy off-market deals with a nice margin of safety right at acquisition.

You will find plenty of regional and national parking operators that specialize in the management of parking lots and garages, and even some publicly traded companies. However, few are actual parking lot asset owners.

Third-party operators have failed to invest specifically in this type of real estate for a long time. Though they could, they focus their business on the management of such structures, choosing to specialize the work they do. They are not in the business of owning real estate. They prefer an asset-light model. They know their core competency lies in managing these properties by incorporating various operational processes that drive up revenue. They earn a percentage of that revenue from the lot owner.

Let's be frank here. There's little doubt that, over the next 10 to 20 years, there will be asset ownership in the industry through the result of consolidation. The key here is to be ahead of the curve. There's plenty of runway opportunity here – a nice way to build value and earn recurring profits for years – before the industry takes off and drives costs higher.

How to Create Profitable Parking Lot Investments

If parking lots are such seemingly easy profits, why isn't everyone else buying them up? While they can provide a nice upgrade in profit margins, there are some tricks to the process.

To start with, location makes a big impact on profitability and even opportunity. Location, as with all aspects of real estate, matters the most here. The only parking lots with a profitable base are those that are paid parking, and the problem is most parking in the U.S. is still free.

To overcome this challenge, we focus just on parking lots that offer a positive cash flow from the first day of ownership. These areas where there is demand for parking are in highly desirable areas, such as in the downtown parts of cities where thousands of people live and work in densely packed areas. When buying parking lots for investment, then, your goal is to find areas with high demand.

High-demand tourist areas are a secondary option. Some areas near larger schools or office centers may also be profitable hotspots. Every city will have its desirable areas – by the waterfront, near a trendy destination location, etc.

The rule is simple: Buy the worst property on the best block. In these areas, where high-rise complexes are located or people fight over street parking, parking lots become premium investment properties.

Invest in Technology to Enhance Operations

Buying the "worst property on the block" doesn't mean you don't have to make any investments in your lots. Rather, it's nearly always beneficial to enhance these locations in simple, but effective methods. New technology, for example, is helping to ensure better operations and driving value up. Placing a sophisticated third-party operator in that lot allows you to drive up revenue by using dynamic pricing models.

The right operator knows their industry and the local market. They are able to use dynamic pricing models to change pricing based on changing market conditions. These are not long-term changes – they change as often as several times a day. During the workday, pricing rises as demand increases. When there's a big event nearby, rents go up as well. With technology in place, it's rather easy to make these adjustments quickly. This helps tremendously in an inflationary environment.

Profitable Pricing Models Benefit Owners, Too

Earlier we noted that we invest in parking lots and then bring aboard parking lot operators to manage them. The lot operators pay rent on a long-term lease. However, because of the flexible pricing models we just discussed, there's also a secondary avenue for income for owners.

Within your contract and lease with the operator, you can create several streams of income. Your first is rent, as noted. Then, there are annual rent escalators and revenue participation above the percentage threshold opportunities.

The third component allows us to take advantage of all of those instances in which the company can drive up costs due to increased demand. There's no additional cost outlay – which means the operator isn't spending anything else. That makes it simple enough to see higher rents when you have an in-demand lot.

Minimize Costs and Overall Maintenance

By comparison, parking lot maintenance is a fraction of the cost of real estate rentals, but there are costs associated with the process nonetheless. This will figure into any business model you create.

Overall, parking lots are low maintenance. You'll need to pay for upkeep on surface lots, which may include pavement patching each year, painting parking lines, and adding bumper blocks. You don't need a lot of capital in hand to own and maintain parking lots. Initially, your biggest cost will be in adding technology to boost profit margin opportunities.

It's even less when you have a third-party operator managing your property. They can be responsible for the entire process including everything from daily cleaning to maintaining parking equipment, advertising mechanisms to draw in customers, and paying for the towing of forgotten vehicles. That reduces your costs even further.

Depreciation and Taxes

Parking lot assets tend to be very affordable in terms of taxation. Much of the initial purchase price, for example, can be allocated to necessary parking lot improvements. This includes the installation of utilities and asphalt. These items depreciate rather quickly in most markets, generally around 15 years. That's almost half of the time associated with residential real estate or a third of the time for commercial property. More so, tax codes in various areas tend to offer bonus depreciation opportunities. The bottom line is, you are not going to pay incredible taxes here.

Worried About a Recession?

Many real estate investments—such as rental property—tend to do well in drops in economic activity. Parking lot assets generally fare well in most recession climates. The demand for parking is always going to be there. If the number of companies drops in a business district, for example, there are still other venues that allow the owner to remain profitable, such as sporting events or nightclubs. Restaurants and entertainment districts, which tend to be right in the heart of busy downtown establishments, have different economic cycles, which helps to keep demand up for parking lots. The income generated is stable and predictable, something every asset owner wants when recession risks rise.

When you employ the use of operators, you further reduce your risks. The operators we use tend to be larger companies with regional or national bases. As a result, when they enter into a contract with us, we often negotiate leases that are guaranteed for five, ten, or more years. That's going to help minimize any recession risk for the property owner, even if demand begins to fall in the area. Operators know their markets—they are not going to agree to these long-term leases unless they know they can handle such turns in the economy.

The Right Exit Strategy

Many parking lot asset owners will want to maintain their ownership for a long time. After all, it is generally a low-risk investment and one with little capital investment, year-after-year. It's the type of long-term, buy-and-hold property that many want.

However, there are various strategies for exiting this industry that can provide a nice boost to your bottom line profits down the road. When buying real estate, you want to buy in up and coming areas--buy low and watch the value grow. The same applies to parking lots. Your covered land play here can really provide peace of mind.

In short, when demand increases for housing or business development, the value of that parking lot grows, not necessarily because of the demand for those spots, though. The value grows as the area becomes more desirable for use as a high-rise condo or an office building.

When you buy in these markets, you are mitigating much of your risk because redevelopment opportunities in the future are high. Right now, you buy the lot and collect on the reliable and consistent rents you are paid on it. That's generating positive cash flow nearly immediately for most asset owners. In the short to medium term, you're seeing steady income.

Later, when you are ready to get out of the market or when the value of selling is simply too high to pass up, you have an opportunity to see a nice disposition price for your parking lot so it can be redeveloped. When development grows in a city, parking lot owners tend to be the first ones called about selling their assets.

Parking lots are that hidden, easy-to-manage asset you simply cannot overlook when enhancing and growing your portfolio. Plenty of investors make their focus on these assets because of the low ongoing risks and the nearly instant positive cash flow.

Here are some recent case studies of parking lot assets we've acquired and the predictable cash flow and passive income for investors involved.

CASE STUDY
DIRECT-TO-OWNER PARKING LOT ACQUISITION

PRINCESS ST PARKING LOT
Wilmington, NC | Off-Market Acquisition | Oct 2020

Overview

The Princess St property is a surface parking lot consisting of 28 spaces in the phenomenal Wilmington MSA. The community was acquired in an off-market transaction, and sourced via our internal direct-to-owner marketing efforts.

About the Project

Upon receiving a direct mail piece, the owner reached out to gauge our interest and was ready to sell in short order. As a doctor, the owner's day job precluded him from appropriately overseeing management of the parking lot. He entrusted his son with day-to-day operations, which led to significant underperformance. He was only generating around $34,000 per year in revenue.

The Challenge

Touting an **exceptional location on a hard signalized corner** in a growing market, the Princess St parking lot has good bones and great fundamentals. That said, poor management resulted in lower-than-expected yields, leaving the owner yearning to cash out. In parking, asset owners have the option to either operate the facility themselves or lease their parking lot to a third-party operator.

The Plan:

Our strategy is to sign favorable long-term NN/NNN leases with credible third party operators capable of generating far more parking revenue than those who self-manage. While negotiating the purchase price with the owner, Sunrise put out a request for bids (RFB) from regional parking lot operators. The most favorable option was to sign a 10-year NN lease, providing base rent of $72,000 annually as well as annual rent escalators to protect the investment from inflation risk.

The Outlook

Knowing in advance how much revenue the property would generate, Sunrise went back to the owner and negotiated a $695k purchase price, which pencils out to a **9.3 capitalization rate** at acquisition. Based on the purchase appraisal of $1mm, we were able to achieve a **43% return on equity** on day one. Our long-term lease provides stable, recurring income for many years into the future. This visibility of income over

THE CASH FLOW INVESTOR

the next decade provides safe, predictable cash flow (and clarity) for our Fund 3 partners.

CASE STUDY

CLEARWATER BEACH, FL PARKING LOT ACQUISITION

NORTH BEACH PARKING PLAZA
Clearwater, FL | Off-Market Acquisition | Aug 2021

**As of March 2022, we're currently working with the City on a public-private partnership to increase the value of the property.

Overview

North Beach Parking Plaza is an institutional grade, Class A property where visitors park to enjoy the #1 beach in the country. The asset was acquired in an off-market, direct-to-owner transaction, and sourced via our network here in the phenomenal Tampa MSA.

About the Project

Touting an exceptional location in a rapidly growing market, North Beach Parking Plaza was newly constructed in 2016 to help offset the massive demand for parking on Clearwater Beach. Developed with a minimum useful life of 40 years, this property should not need any major capital expenditures for years to come.

The Challenge

Real Estate Investing is all about Location, Location, Location. This prime piece of property sits on the main shopping corridor of one of the best beaches in the world. That said, a disgruntled partnership amongst owners led the original developer down the path of selling. Immediately upon hearing the asset may come available, we reached out to the owner and put the property under contract before it hit the open market.

The Plan:

We intend to buy, improve, and hold for North Beach Parking Plaza for decades to come. It's a generational asset on Clearwater Beach that will provide stable, recurring income for many years into the future. This visibility of income provides safe, predictable cash flow (and clarity) for our Fund 3 partners.

The Outlook

Based on the purchase appraisal, Sunrise immediately created over $1.5mm built-in sweat equity at acquisition. We were able to lock in multiple years of interest-only financing with a 300 basis-point spread on an institutional-grade, Class A property. This is truly a generational asset that will help hundreds of accredited investors earn passive income and build legacy wealth over time.

SECTION IV
STARTING YOUR JOURNEY

CHAPTER 15
INVESTING WITH A PURPOSE

Anyone can invest—but to be truly successful and keep pushing forward, you need to invest with a purpose. Ultimately, that comes down to finding YOUR unique "why," carving a path to your niche and, once you've succeeded, giving back to the community and helping make the world a better place.

Real estate investing isn't just a great way to drive long-term revenue—it's also a purpose-driven way to create the life that serves *your why.* Beyond being a massive money-maker, real estate investing can and should be as individual as you, anchored in what you're interested in, what you believe in and how you want to spend your time, talent and resources. In other words, you want to invest with a purpose.

Revisiting Your "Why"

There are countless ways to create wealth. What's important, though, is creating wealth on *your* terms.

This, ultimately, goes back to your "why." Why are you doing this, specifically? In Chapter One, I explained my why—my family and my kids—and *that* is what steers me as a real estate investor. They are the reason I get out of bed every single day. They are the reason I hustle from the minute I wake up until the minute my head hits the pillow at night.

Maybe your "why" is family, too, or maybe it's something else. Maybe you want to retire comfortably and travel the world without thinking twice about your bank account. Maybe you simply want to quit your 9-to-5. Whatever your reason, it's important you come back to that in determining your purpose and how you want to move forward. Often your "why" will determine your next steps—the niche you ultimately choose and how you structure your real estate investing business.

Moving Beyond The Money

That path from your "why" to your real estate investing niche is truly personal and unique for each investor. Again, there are countless ways to create wealth. If you've determined your "why" and decided that real estate investing will help you achieve your goals, it's important to figure out the right specific path—what type of investing is the ideal fit. Find this, and you'll be better positioned to go the distance—to stick with real estate investing for the long haul, growing your business and building your wealth so you can achieve your goals.

That's the dream, and that's the *true* goal of building your real estate investing business. Find something that directly aligns with you as an individual—something you enjoy doing that can help you achieve the lifestyle you're craving. That's all. It's as simple as it is complex. It all comes back to your "why."

The Importance Of Giving Back

If you find your "why," lock into your niche and start your journey towards real estate investing wealth, you'll be making meaningful strides soon enough. If your "why" is providing for your family, pretty soon you'll be covering their expenses and, likely, being able to fund those "extras"—the dinners out, the new house, the trips, whatever sits beyond the basics. That's a good feeling. That's empowering.

Soon enough, you'll reach another point. Now, you have *more* than you need to cover your general living expenses and the overall lifestyle you've always wanted. You and your family are comfortable, secure and able to weather even a serious financial storm. There's no stress. There's no worry. There's no wondering where that money is going to come from. You can just live. And you still have extra cash coming in.

At that point, give back. Use your success and the wealth that ensues to make the world a better place. There are endless ways to do this, whether you give money to charities, lend a helping hand in your community, fund a project or lift up a person in need. Like aligning with the right real estate investing path, it's essential to find the right way to give back.

How We're Investing In The Community

I, personally, like to give back to a number of charitable organizations. We participate in a charitable bike ride we put on annually, called the *"72-Hours to Key West Charity Bike Ride"*. Every year, I get to couple my passion for cycling with my passion for giving back to the community, in a three-day, 280-mile epic adventure. Seeing this ride in action is awe-inspiring—it's just amazing. I've been committed to this initiative for well over a decade, and I don't see it stopping anytime soon.

Many of our employees and people in our extended network participate, raising hundreds of thousands of dollars for two foundations close to my heart, *The Tiny Hands Foundation* and *Starting Right, Now.*

For us, it's not just about the money—far from it. It's about supporting future generations. It's about using our wealth and success to create a better world, starting with our immediate universe.

Granted, like any business, we *also* invest profits in our own growth and evolution—that's equally essential. If you don't use your profits to grow your business, you won't be in business for long. That said, you can and should use extra resources and energy to improve and enhance your community and the world beyond your front door. That's what we do and that's what we'll *always* do, ideally deepening our commitment and our contributions as we go. I encourage YOU to do the same.

CHAPTER 16
YOUR NEXT STEP

Are you ready to set the wheels in motion and get started investing and building your portfolio?

One of the biggest challenges in the real estate investing process is getting started. Even if you "get it," even if you're excited to get started, even if this has been your dream for decades, setting those all-important wheels in motion is still, likely, a hurdle standing between you and your future successes. And that's a problem. Fortunately, it's a simple problem to overcome. The secret: think big then act small.

If it sounds counterintuitive, think of it this way. At this point, you no doubt understand the big picture of what you're going to do and why you're going to do it. But now, you need to put one foot in front of the other so you can achieve your goals and build your business.

Start Here: Plan For Five Years From Now

The first step is to flesh out your five-year plan. This is the *easiest* thing to do because you have a sense of where you want to be and why. That becomes the foundation of your initial planning.

Looking at the grid below, think about where you are today and try to envision what you want to accomplish in the next five years.

	TODAY	5 YEARS
Total Income		
Total Passive Income		
Average Hours Worked/ Week		
Weeks of Vacation/Year		
# of Real Estate Deals in Portfolio		
Other_____		
Other_____		
Other_____		

For each of the items above, fill in your *current* status—i.e. how much income you earn right now and how many hours you work per week—then fill in your ideal for five years from now. If you don't know, make your best guess. You want to be within the realm of possibility but, still, think big. For example, wanting to generate $1,000,000 in a single year is doable, especially if you stay the course for the next five years. Saying you want to generate $100 *billion,* though, likely isn't. Don't set yourself up to fail. Be smart and strategic when developing your five-year financial goals but, at the same time, think BIG.

Next, give some thought to what your typical day would ideally look like five years from now. If, for example, you're slaving away at a 9-to-5, you may know that you don't want that in the future. You may want to get your kids at school every day or coach soccer or never have to travel for work again. You might want to eat dinner with your spouse every night, or travel for the entire summer, every summer.

Ultimately, only you can answer those questions. Give some thought to your "perfect" life based on the income parameters you've outlined above, then answer the following questions:

- What do you do for an income? Do you invest in real estate exclusively?

- What time do you wake up in the morning?

- Do you have any hobbies or interests? How and when do you pursue them?

- On a scale of 1-10, with 10 being "very stressed" and 1 being "not stressed at all," how would you rate your stress level on a typical day?

- What does a typical day look like?

- Where do you go?

- Who do you meet with?

- Who do you eat meals with?

- How much time do you spend "working?"

- How often do you travel or pursue your passions?

- What is the best part of your "new" life five years from now?

Breaking Down Your Five-Year Plan

Once your five-year plan is established, it's time to start breaking it down into manageable, actionable pieces—things you can do *right now* to get your real estate investing in motion. To do that, you'll want to establish a *12-month roadmap*.

Establishing a one-year plan is very simple now that you have the framework in place from your five-year overview. First, start with your financial goals. If, for example, you want to make $25,000 per month in passive income within five years, you can start backing into what your portfolio would need to look like. Depending on your market, that could mean 25 properties, each with a positive cash flow of $1,000 per month. It could also mean 100 with $250 cash flow per month.

Thinking about your market, your niche and your property management goals, you can likely refine that view. For example, if you're investing in higher-end condos on the beach, generating $1,000 per unit in positive cash flow is absolutely doable. If you're building up in a more rural community or an area with lower rents, you may be looking at $100 to $250 per month in positive cash flow—and *that* could mean taking on an apartment building or other space with more units and more cash flow potential from the beginning.

Let's say yours is a higher end market with beautiful, sought-after condo communities commanding $2,500 to $3,000 per month—and you want in. Each unit represents $1,000 in positive cash flow, meaning you'd need 25 of these properties—or similar cash flow properties—to get to your goal of $25,000 in monthly passive income. Now break that down. To get to 25 purchases, you'll need to invest in at least five properties in year one. After that, you'll add five or more per year until you cross the 25-property finish line.

Granted, your goals don't need to be consistent for the next five years. Maybe you want to get to 25 properties, but feel more comfortable investing in one to two per year. If that case, you may set buying *two* properties as your goal for the next 12 months, then expand your portfolio as the years go on.

Thinking about this, what do you want to accomplish in the next 12 months to boost your real estate investing business?

SETTING SMART GOALS

As you evaluate your 12-month goals, ask yourself, "are these SMART goals?"

- **S**pecific
- **M**easurable
- **A**ttainable
- **R**elevant
- **T**ime-bound

Evaluating your next steps against "SMART" criteria will help you set better, more meaningful and more achievable goals—goals that you'll be able to meet *and* goals that will drive you and your business forward.

Let's take an example. If you decide you want to invest in *five* luxury condos in the next 12 months, write that down—then ask yourself how you can make it SMART:

ORIGINAL STATEMENT: I want to make money by investing in real estate.

SMART STATEMENT: I want to invest in five luxury condos generating at least $1,000 in positive cash flow per month—and each within 20 miles of my home—by December 31.

Getting Down to the Quarters

While it's easier to map out one year than it is five, 12 months from now can feel like an eternity, and that can keep you from taking action today. The next step is to break your yearly goal into four quarterly goals.

Thinking about what you'll accomplish in the next 90 days feels more attainable and will, ideally, drive you to take more decisive, more immediate action.

In this scenario, we want five luxury condos in our portfolio by the end of the year—so what does that look like quarter to quarter? Will you spend the next three months "growing" your business, or will you take action and actually invest in a condo—or even *two*—within the next three months? The choice is yours, but seeing it on paper will, no doubt, help you along.

My advice is to aim to complete one investment in your first 90 days, if at all possible. That likely means finding your first investment property fairly soon, but that's OK. You have the tools, resources and overarching foundation you need to be successful. Now it's time to put it all to use.

Thinking about your own yearly goal, explain what each *quarterly goal* looks like for the next four quarters. Ask yourself:

> *What do you want to do three months from now?*
>
> *What do you want to do six months from now?*
>
> *What do you want to do nine months from now?*
>
> *What do you want to do twelve months from now?*

Remember, put your goals through the "SMART" lens to ensure they make sense for you and your business. Don't worry about how you'll get to these mini-finish lines just yet. For now, focus on where you want to be in 90 days.

Break it Down Week-by-Week

Now you've done it—you've established clear-cut goals for the next three months, the next 12 months and the next *five years*. That should feel good and should give you a real sense of forward momentum. You see a path and, now, all you have to do is follow it.

To ensure you stay the course—and to maximize your chance of success—you need to create a weekly workflow that *works*. This will be different for everyone. What I do every week might be completely different from your process, and that's perfectly fine. The point is to stay the course and keep moving forward.

Keep in mind that these "processes" are all workflows, actions and tasks that help guide your success as a real estate investor and that, together, help move you towards your quarterly, yearly and five-year objectives. They may seem insignificant on their own, but they're about taking steps to improve your intel, your insights and your actions taken. Some examples:

- Attend at least one industry or networking event per week
- See at least five properties per week
- Analyze two deals per day
- Spend 30 minutes per day on the MLS
- Use your commute time to listen to real estate investing podcasts
- Read 15 pages of a real estate investing book per day

These are just examples but, as you can see, they're "SMART" and you can dig into them *right now*. Each will make you a better real estate investor but, together, you'll gain the information and the discipline you need to push yourself ahead.

Your Weekly Deal Funnel

Regardless of the action items you choose, you'll *definitely* want to add "deal funnel" to your weekly list. A deal funnel is exactly what it sounds like: a funnel of deals. At the top of the funnel are new and prospective leads—leads you're batting around or that you somehow discovered and may consider as an investment deal.

As leads move down the funnel, more and more drop out of investment contention—and that's a good thing. At each stage of the funnel, you're taking some action to determine if *this* is the right deal for your business—and if it's not, you're cutting it loose.

Every week you want to make sure the top of your lead is *full*—and that will mean different things to different investors. You may discover you need 20 quality leads at the top of your funnel to close a single deal, or you need three to five. It all depends on your investing niche and your market.

With leads in your funnel, you can move into the next stage: analyze. Analyze each of the prospects and determine which might make sense—which are in the right location, in the right price range and are, ultimately, ones *you* want to invest in.

Sometimes this process is simple—if you only want to invest in luxury condos right now, there's probably very little chance a parking lot or warehouse will drive you to invest. But, sometimes, you'll be on the fence about a property and need more insights and information. Those may require an in-person visit, another call to the seller or some deep digging by your investor-friendly real estate agent.

The properties that seem to be in-line, then, move to the next stage: propose. In the "propose" stage, you'll make offers on the properties that check out. As you're determining what to bid on, be sure you're being smart, strategic and not wasting your time. If you analyzed a property to be worth $110,000 and the owner wants $350,000 for it, you likely won't find common ground—and likely won't be able to convince them your offer is competitive and market-driven.

However, if you determine a property is worth $110,000 and they're asking $130,000, have at it. Maybe simply walking them through your process, offering a cash close and covering their closing costs or throwing in some low- or no-cost extra—finding them a rental, for example—could get the deal *done*.

Those deals, then, move into the "close" stage. You'll start to see trends. Maybe you close 10% of every deal that hits the top of your funnel, or maybe it's closer to 5%. Maybe your market is ripe for investing but incredibly underserved, and you can close virtually every property that crosses your inbox. Maybe there's a ton of competition and you need 50 properties at the top of your funnel at any given time.

You'll quickly see how far ahead you need to be to meet your goals and, from there, can maintain a better, more efficient meeting. This should be a *weekly* task. Keep the top of your funnel full and keep moving those properties through each day. Don't let leads linger at the top. If you've spotted it, so have other savvy investors and, chances are, they're moving quickly to analyze, propose and close.

Time Block Out Your Day

With these larger goals and objectives established, you are likely seeing a path to achievement. Now it's time to break everything into daily goals and objectives so you know exactly what to do every single day.

Personally, I've found time blocking to be very effective. Each day, break your time into chunks—it could be by the hour or 30-minute increments. You could even break the work day into "morning," "afternoon" and "late afternoon" if you need more flexibility.

Once you've divided your day into these blocks, assign a specific task to those times. Ideally, start with the toughest or least desirable task first so you can get through it and move on. After that, the rest of your tasks should seem like a breeze.

You will need to be highly accountable. At the end of each day, review your original time-blocked schedule and see where you excelled and where you fell short. Could you add more to your day? Did a specific task hold you up more than anticipated? How can you better allocate your time, talent and resources *next week?*

Soon enough, you'll find your rhythm and be able to structure your day in a meaningful way. For now, be sure you're time blocking and checking yourself against your daily goals to see what's working and what's not— and, equally important, that each task feeds into your weekly goals. Done right, you will get to those goals and work your way closer and closer to your five year plan.

FINAL THOUGHTS

So… we're here at the end of, what I hope was an exciting, enlightening, and actionable journey towards a more financially independent future. From here, all you need to do is put your foot on the gas—and keep it there. Because now your job is to apply what you've learned over these last few chapters.

Now it's your chance to go out and find opportunity—because, as you can see, it's everywhere. Go build an incredible passive income stream so you can generate revenue from anywhere, anytime, whether you're working on your business or not.

Go live. Enjoy your friends. Enjoy your family. Find things that bring you joy and do them—because, now, you'll have the time and resources to pursue any path you want.

Go and give back. Like I'm working to pay it forward, I want you to do the same. As you start to grow and scale your business, think about how you can help others who are in the same spot you're in right now. How can you mentor them? Show them the ropes? Help them on their journey forward?

As I'm sure you can see, creating a meaningful passive income stream through commercial real estate investing isn't just possible, it's simple.

If you apply this newfound knowledge and commit to taking a step forward—then another, then another—you'll have a thriving real estate investing business sooner than you can even imagine. I did it, and now it's your turn.

This book is just a piece of what should be feeding that journey forward. Consider what you've learned here to be the foundation—and now it's time to build from the ground up. I encourage you to use the tools and resources included here to ensure your path is smooth, seamless, and successful—basically, everything I wish I had when I was starting out.

This includes:

1. Tune in to the Real Estate Investing for Cash Flow Podcast

If you feel like your passive income opportunity is limited, make this your first stop. In the *Real Estate Investing for Cash Flow with Kevin Bupp* podcast, you'll find hundreds of one-on-one interviews with some of the most innovative business executives, real estate investors and thought leaders who have mastered countless paths to creating passive income streams and legacy wealth. Check out the main podcast page at www. KevinBupp.com/podcast.

2. Learn More About the Mobile Home Park Academy

Mobile Home Parks are one of the most profitable niches of real estate investing, and I'm excited to share my passion for investing in them with you. If you're ready to dive into mobile home park investing, our *Mobile Home Park Academy* packages up everything you need to get started right away. The Mobile Home Park Academy is an in-depth, online program that provides investors with the exact blueprint and necessary hands-on training to run their own successful mobile home park. The MHP Academy is available at www.KevinBupp.com/mhpacademy.

3. Invest Alongside Me and My Team at Sunrise Capital Investors

Are you interested in being a passive investor, without being involved with managing assets? Become a passive investor with me and my team.

At Sunrise, we specifically focus on low-risk, cash flowing assets that generate capital protection, immediate passive income, and equity growth for our investor partners. Our unique strategies allow us to buy, improve, and hold assets that in turn help you generate cash flow & legacy wealth. Go here to learn more: www.KevinBupp.com/invest.

4. Book a Speaking Engagement

In addition to virtual resources, I speak at corporate events, retreats, and conferences. To book Kevin for your next event, go to www.KevinBupp.com/speak.

5. Bring Kevin a Deal

I'm actively looking to purchase mobile home parks, parking lots and parking garages nationwide, and I need your help in doing so. So if you bring us an off-market deal that meets our criteria and we purchase it, you can earn anywhere between $50,000 to $200,000 in finders' fees for your efforts. This is a great way that we can make money together! Go to www.BringKevinADeal.com for more information.

6. Download the Investors Resource Bundle

I've helped many aspiring investors generate cash flow and build wealth through commercial real estate, and I've compiled some of my best and most essential resources into one ultimate resource bundle—all for free—for you. This bundle includes:

- The Passive Investor's Guide to Mobile Park Investing, an eBook that covers the ins and outs of how you can buy, improve, and hold mobile home parks to help you generate cash flow.

- I've seen inexperienced investors make some truly terrible mistakes that have cost them hundreds of thousands of dollars. Mistakes that could've been easily avoidable if they had the right knowledge and education. My eBook, The 21 Biggest Mistakes Investors Make When Buying Their First Mobile Home Park… And How To Avoid Them digs deep into some of these common mistakes—helping you avoid them, and cutting years off your learning curve. Trust me, you want this.

- We invest for cash flow and legacy wealth. So to avoid outsized risk, it's important to acquire assets that have positive cash flow in place from day one. My Mobile Home Park Deal Analyzer is a very simple, very useful interactive spreadsheet that enables you to quickly analyze any real estate deal that comes across your desk—so you can quickly decide if the deal is worth your time… in 10 minutes or less.

- I've also included my Passive Investor's Guide to Parking Lot Profits. The demand for parking is massive, and this report is designed to show you how you can make huge profits from investing in this niche.

- When reaching out to potential sellers and inquiring about buying their asset, you can't afford to just wing it. You need a properly structured script. Through the years, and over the course of tons of phone calls, I've developed and refined an effective Cold Calling Script. This script is short and simple—and proven to work time and time again no matter what part of the country I invest in. I use this same script every day in my own business to gauge seller motivation, make personal connections, and initiate sellers to move forward.

- Lastly, download my Letter of Intent (LOI) template. Drafting a letter of intent can be tricky: while it does have legal ramifications, it's not always legally binding. Let me share with you our standard LOI section by section so you know where the legal landmines are buried. Customize it to make your own—and there will be nothing holding you back from making an offer on your next great deal.

Get immediate access to the full resource bundle here:
www.KevinBupp.com/freebundle.

ACKNOWLEDGEMENTS

They say it takes a village to raise a child, and in many ways writing a book like this takes a village. I am both humbled and eternally grateful to all those who personally supported me through my real estate journey, and who have supported this book. It is impossible to thank everyone who's made an impact on my life throughout these last twenty years of my Real Estate escapades, but there are a few people who deserve specific mention.

My beautiful wife, Joanna, and our two boys, Jackson and Julian, are at the very top of that list. Joanna and I met in 2008, right about the time my financial world was crumbling during the great recession. She was there by my side offering endless support no matter how rough the road got….and believe me, those were some trying times. Without Joanna's selfless support and unconditional love, I wouldn't be the man I am today. And to my two incredibly charming boys (Jackson and Julian), you two are my 'Why' and make me want to be the best version of myself each and every day.

Next on this list is my business partner, Brian Spear. Thank you my friend for being the driving force that got this book to the finish line. You simply get shit done and without you this book might have never been published. I am forever grateful for your friendship and the business that we've built together. GO BIG BLUE!

To the man that introduced me to the real estate game some 20+ years ago—David Christmas. Simply put, I'm not sure I would have ever found Real Estate if it wasn't for you. Thank you for your mentorship , friendship, and unwavering support. To the friend and mentor that helped me 'Dream Big' and elevate my business to a much greater level – Rod Khleif.

Scott Myers, Gene Guarino (RIP my friend), and Rod Khleif – thank you all for your generous contributions and support for this book.

I would also like to acknowledge numerous instrumental teammates who have made this book possible. I have been privileged to work with Keisha Cross, Ariana Klugiewicz, Megan O'Malley, Amber Vilhauer, Ashley Bunting, Carlos Terrazas, Alex Gallegos, and Karla Pollorena amongst others. All provided enthusiastic assistance, working tirelessly throughout the journey to get published. The mission has been to make an impact by helping as many readers as possible achieve financial freedom. If you find this book useful, they deserve an enormous amount of credit.

Lastly, to my tribe of Cash Flow Investors, thank you for your many years of continued support and continued belief in me. You know who you are.

GLOSSARY OF TERMS

While you'll learn as you go in the commercial real estate investing industry, it's good to have a foundation of terms, phrases and keywords that are common to the process.

Some of the following definitions are adapted from these sources: "NAIOP Commercial Real Estate Development Development Association – Industry Terms and Definitions," retrieved February 2022 from: https://www.naiop.org/Education-and-Career/Industry-Terms-and-Definitions, and the Realtors Commercial Alliance—Glossary of Commercial Real Estate Terms, retrieved February 2022 from http://www.naiophouston.org/pdf/development/TERMS-REAL_ESTATE_COMPLETE.pdf, and the "Boxer's Glossary of Commercial Real Estate Terms," retrieved February 2022 from: https://www.boxerproperty.com/cre-glossary.

Accredited Investor

Individual or business entity that is allowed to invest in certain investment opportunities based on satisfying at least one requirement regarding their income, net worth, asset size, governance status, or professional experience.

Actual Rate of Return

Formula that reflects the actual gain or loss of an investment over a certain period of time compared to the initial investment's cost. This is the preferred way to measure actual returns on investments because it isn't based on an average percentage but rather on the actual investment return compared to the original cost. Beware of "average" rate of return, which can be misleading.

Acquisition

Refers to purchasing existing properties, operating them, and then reselling them to others

Amortization

The repayment of loan principal through equal payments over a designated period of time consisting of both principal and interest.

"As-Is" Condition

The acceptance by the tenant of the premises in their existing condition at the time the lease is executed. This would include acceptance of any physical defects, code violations, or other problems with the physical and legal condition of the premises.

Asset Cash Flow

The aggregate total of all cash flows related to the assets of a business. This information is used to determine the net amount of cash being spun off by or used in the operations of a business.

Asset Type

Also known as the "property category" this is the classification of commercial real estate based on its primary use. Primary asset types are multi-family, retail, office, land, hospitality, mixed use, industrial and special purpose.

Asset Class

A group of investment types with similar characteristics and subject to the same laws, regulations, and market forces. Each group is usually defined as Class A, Class B or Class C property, with Class A representing the highest quality and Class C representing the lowest quality. Classes are based on a combination of different factors, including property age, property location, rental income, appreciation, amenities, and more.

Assessed Value

The value of real property established by the tax assessor for the purpose of levying real estate taxes.

Assignment

The transfer of an one party's rights or property to another person or business. This option exists in a variety of business transactions. For investors, the most prominent example occurs when a purchase sale agreement (PSA) is assigned; the assignee has an obligation to complete the requirements of the contract. Other business transactions are also known as an assignment.

Average Annual Effective Rate

The average annual effective rent divided by the square footage.

Average Annual Effective Rent

The tenant's total effective rent divided by the lease term.

Average Rate of Return

A formula that reflects the percentage rate of return on an investment or asset compared to the initial investment's cost. Be careful because this average can be misleading and doesn't necessarily reflect the actual rate of return.

Basis

The total amount paid for a property, including equity capital and the amount of debt incurred.

Basis Points (BPs) Values equal to one-hundredth of one percentage point. For example, 100 basis points = 1 percentage point.

Bridge Loan

Short-term financing used until a person or company secures permanent financing or removes an existing obligation. Bridge loans are short-term, typically up to one year.

Broker

A real estate agent who represents a principal party and facilitates the buying, selling, or leasing of commercial property.

Building Class

Building classes refer to the desirability of location, modernization of the building, types of amenities, age, and some other factors. Buildings are rated as Class A, Class B, Class C and Class D.

Business Risk

The uncertainty associated with the possible profit outcomes of a business venture.

Buyer

The individual, group, company, or entity that has purchased a commercial real estate asset.

Cash-on-cash Rate

A return measure that is calculated as cash flow before taxes divided by the initial equity investment.

Capital Expenses or Cap Ex

Improvements (as opposed to repairs) to a fixed asset that will increase the value or useful life of that asset. A capital expenditure is typically amortized or depreciated over the useful life of the asset, as opposed to a repair, which is expensed in the year incurred.

Capital Improvements

Any addition or alteration to real property that meets one of the following conditions: It substantially adds to the value of the real property or appreciably prolongs the useful life of the real property.

Capital Partner

All partners who have contributed capital to the partnership. Often this phrase is referring to the partner that contributed the most capital to a partnership.

Capitalization Rate (Cap Rate)

Also referred to as "cap rate", this is a percentage that relates the value of an income-producing property to its future income, expressed as net operating income (NOI) divided by purchase price.

Cash Flow

The amount of income earned from investments and other assets. The net cash received in any period, taking into account net operating income, debt service, capital expenses, loan proceeds, sale revenues, and any other sources and uses of cash.

Cash Flow Investing

Cash flow derived from assets or investments that is paid on an ongoing and regular basis. Typically, distributions or interest payments are paid quarterly or monthly.

Cash-On-Cash Return

Cash on cash return is also known as your ROI, or return on investment. It is the heart of your money or your investor's money and is basically your annual cash flow divided by your down payment.

Class A Building

Class A buildings are the newest and highest quality, with the best location and highest rents. Class A is the most desirable of the asset classes.

Class B Building

Class B buildings are usually a little older, but they are still good quality and attract average, working class tenants. Class B is the second most desirable of the asset classes.

Class C Building

Class C is the lowest official classification and the buildings are older and need updating. They have the lowest rents and you'll find lower to middle income tenants in them. Class C is the third most desirable of the asset classes.

Class D Building

These buildings are often vacant and in need of extensive renovation.

Crowdfunding

The practice of funding a project or venture by raising small amounts of money from a large number of people, typically via the internet. Crowdfunding is a form of crowdsourcing and alternative finance.

Deal Flow

A term used by investors, investment bankers, and venture capitalists to describe the rate at which business proposals and investment pitches are being received.

Deal Structure

The agreement reached in financing an acquisition. The deal can be unleveraged, leveraged, traditional debt, participating debt, participating/convertible debt, or a joint venture, among other things.

Debt Coverage Ratio (DCR)

The debt coverage ratio is the amount of cash flow available to pay the mortgage payment. It's the ratio of the net operating income (NOI) to the mortgage payment.

Formula: DCR = NOI / Annual Debt

Deed

A legal document used to convey the transfer of a real estate asset from the seller to the buyer.

Default

Failure to fulfill an obligation, especially with regards to repayment of a loan.

Demand

The volume or quantity of a product or service purchased, or willing to be purchased, in relation to price.

Demographics

Characteristics of human populations as defined by population size and density of regions, population growth rates, migration, vital statistics, and their effect on socio-economic conditions.

Depreciation

The loss of utility and value of a property.

Discount Rate

Interest rate used in discounted cash flow (DCF) analysis to determine the present value of future cash flows.

Discounted Effective Rent

The cash flows over the term of the lease, discounted to the present value.

Diversification

A method of reducing risk by investing in unrelated (uncorrelated) assets.

Due Diligence

The process of examining a property, related documents, and procedures conducted by or for the potential lender or purchaser to reduce risk. Applying a consistent standard of inspection and investigation one can determine if the actual conditions do or do not reflect the information as represented.

Easements

Rights to use land for a specific purpose

Engineering Reports

An engineering report will confirm all structural elements of a property including the foundation, wood rot, soil erosion and other major structural issues. This can help unearth current and future issues.

Environmental Reports

Formal reports drawn up by an environmental engineer to confirm past and current uses that could impact the soil, air, water or other environmental elements.

Equity Investment

A financial transaction where a certain number of shares of a given company or fund are bought, entitling the owner to be compensated ratably according to his ownership percentage. Typically referred to as shareholders' equity (or owner's equity for privately held companies), an individual or company invest money into a private or public company to become a shareholder.

Escrow

A legal concept describing a financial instrument whereby an asset or escrow money is held by a third party on behalf of two other parties that are in the process of completing a transaction.

Feasibility Analysis

The process of evaluating a proposed project to determine if that project will satisfy the objectives set forth by the agents involved (including owners, investors, developers, and lessees).

Fiduciary

A person or organization that acts on behalf of another person or persons, putting their clients' interests ahead of their own, with a duty to preserve good faith and trust. Being a fiduciary requires being bound both legally and ethically to act in the other's best interests. It also involves trust, especially with regard to the relationship between a trustee and a beneficiary, always having the beneficiary's best interest at heart.

Financial Risk

The possible change in an investment's ability to return principal and income

Fixed Expenses

Costs that do not change with a building's occupancy rate. They include property taxes, insurance, and some forms of building maintenance.

Future Value (FV)

The amount to which money grows over a designated period of time at a specified rate of interest.

Gross Operating Income

The total income generated by the operations of a property before payment of operating expenses. It is calculated from potential rental income, plus other income affected by vacancy, less vacancy and credit losses, plus other income not affected by vacancy. The Annual Property Operating Data form or the Cash Flow Analysis Worksheet can be used to calculate a property's gross operating income.

Gross Rent Multiplier (GRM)

A method investors may use to determine market value. Used to measure and compare a property's potential valuation by dividing the price of the property by its gross income. This is a good method for identifying properties with low asking price compared to market-driven revenue potential.

Hard Money Loan

A loan that is secured by real property and considered a loan of "last resort" or short-term bridge loan. It is primarily used in real estate transactions, with the lender generally being individuals or companies and not banks.

Hedging

Protecting oneself against negative outcomes.

Highest and best use

The reasonably probable and legal use of vacant land or an improved property, which is physically possible, appropriately supported, financially feasible, and that results in the highest value.

Income Capitalization Approach

A method to estimate the value of an income-producing property by converting net operating income into a value. The cap rate is divided into the net operating income to obtain the estimated value. Value = net operating income ÷ capitalization rate

Internal Rate of Return (IRR)

For income properties, it is the interest or discount rate needed to discount the sum of future net cash flows, including amortization and payments of loans and depreciation of the real property, to an amount equal to the initial equity of the property.

Investment Value

The value to a specific investor, based on that investor's requirements, tax rate, or financing.

Landlord

The owner of a property that is rented or leased to a tenant.

Letter of Intent (LOI)

LOI is an acronym for "Letter of Intent," which is a document that expresses the intent of each party in a real estate agreement. It is not a legally binding contract, but it is aimed at reducing misunderstandings between the parties.

Lien

A legal claim against an asset used to secure a loan that must be paid when the property is sold. Liens can be structured in many different ways. In some cases, the creditor will have a legal claim against an asset but not actually hold it in possession, while in other cases the creditor will actually hold on to the asset until the debt is paid off. The former is a more common arrangement when the asset is productive since the creditor would prefer that the asset be used to produce a stream of income to pay off debt rather than just held in possession and not used

Loan to Value Ratio (LTV)

The ratio between a mortgage loan and the value of the property pledged as security, usually expressed as a percentage.

THE CASH FLOW INVESTOR

Market Rent

A rental rate that a property would command on the open real estate market.

Net Cash Flow

Net cash flow is the annual income produced by an investment property after deducting allowances for capital repairs, leasing commissions, tenant inducements (after the initial lease is up) and debt service from net operating income.

Net Lease

A lease in which the tenant pays, in addition to rent, all operating expenses such as real estate taxes, insurance premiums, and maintenance costs.

Net Operating Income (NOI)

The income generated after deducting operating expenses but before deducting taxes and financing expenses. The net operating income calculation is NOI is equal to your gross rental income minus your expenses.

Off-Market Transactions

An investment that has not been advertised publicly for sale, so there is no competition or less competition to buy the asset

Operating Agreement

A key document used by an LLC because it outlines the business financial and functional decisions, including rules, regulations, and provisions. It

274

governs the internal operations of the business in a way that suits the specific needs of the business owners.

Operating Company

A business that produces goods or services and has regular operations.

Operating Expenses

Cash outlays necessary to operate and maintain a property. Examples of operating expenses include real estate taxes, property insurance, property management and maintenance expenses, utilities, and legal or accounting expenses. Operating expenses do not include capital expenditures, debt service, or cost recovery.

Passive Income

Income received from investments and other assets that requires little to no effort to earn and maintain. This is one of the lowest taxed incomes.

Personal Guarantee

An individual's legal promise to repay credit issued to a business for which they serve as an executive or partner.

Principal

The original sum of money borrowed in a loan or put into an investment.

Private Equity

An alternative investment class that consists of capital and is not listed on a public exchange. It is comprised of funds of investors who directly invest in private companies or that engage in buyouts of public companies, resulting in the delisting of public equity

Private Placement Memorandum (PPM)

A legal document provided to prospective investors when selling stock or another security in a business. It is sometimes referred to as an offering memorandum or offering document.

Profits Interest

An equity right based on the future value of a partnership awarded to an individual for their services to the partnership. The reward consists of receiving a percentage of profits from a partnership without having to contribute capital.

Property Manager

A company or an individual responsible for the day-to-day and who oversees all operational aspects of a building. Once a tenant signs a lease, it is the Property Manager who will assist the tenant with any questions, the build-out of the space, and any on-going issues once they have moved in.

Purchase Sale Agreement (PSA)

The document received after mutual acceptance of an offer. It states the final sale price and all terms of the purchase.

Rate of Return

The percentage return on each dollar invested. Also known as yield.

Real Estate Fund

A mutual fund that primarily focuses on investing in securities offered by public real estate companies.

Real Estate Investment Trust (REIT)

A company that owns, operates, or finances income-generating real estate. Modeled after mutual funds, REITs pool the capital of numerous investors. They make it possible for individual investors to earn dividends from real estate investments without having to buy, manage, or finance any properties themselves.

Recapitalization

A term used when owners liquidate some or most of their ownership position in an asset by selling some or most of their equity position.

Return on Investment (ROI)

A performance measure used to evaluate the efficiency of an investment or compare the efficiency of a number of different investments. The ROI tries to directly measure the amount of return on a particular investment relative to the investment's cost. The benefit (or return) of an investment is divided by the cost of the investment to calculate ROI. The result is expressed as a percentage or a ratio.

Right of First Refusal

The right of a party to match the terms of a proposed contract with another party. Also known as first right of refusal

Sales Price

The total amount paid for a property at a particular point in time.

Sales Comparison Approach

A way to determine market value by comparing a subject property to properties with the same or similar characteristics.

Seller

An individual, group, company, or entity that sells a commercial real estate asset.

Seller Finance Loan

A real estate agreement in which the seller handles the mortgage process instead of a financial institution. The buyer signs a mortgage with the seller instead of applying for a conventional bank mortgage. Also called owner financing or seller carry

Stabilized Cap Rate

A stabilized cap rate is the ratio between the net operating income produced by a property upon achieving target occupancy, and its purchase value

Structure

The relationship between the specific investment terms in an agreement.

Structural Repairs

Major repairs to things like a property's roof or foundation; these are often costly and time consuming.

Syndication

A partnership between several investors to combine skills, resources, and capital to purchase and manage a property they otherwise couldn't afford.

Mechanical Repairs

Major repairs to things like plumbing systems, HVAC, water/sewage and other costly mechanical systems.

Tenant

A person, business, or group that pays rent to an owner or landlord for the right to use/occupy a property or space.

Title

A title is the bundled rights tied to a piece of property, of which a party owns a legal interest or equitable interest. A title can also refer to a deed or other legal document that proves ownership.

Triple Net Lease

A lease agreement whereby the tenant pays taxes, maintenance and property insurance as well as all operating costs associated with the tenant's occupancy, including personal property taxes, janitorial services and all utility costs. The landlord is responsible for the roof and the structure and sometimes the parking lot

Survey

A comprehensive assessment and visual of land or a property; this shows boundaries and borders, plus major property features

Vacancy Rate

A measurement expressed as a percentage of the total amount of vacant space divided by the total amount of inventory. This measurement is typically applied to a building, a submarket or a market.

Value Add Investment

An investment in a real estate asset with existing cash flow (and value) that can be increased by raising occupancy, rents or both. Owners typically carry out one or more of the following to add value to a building: improve or replace building systems, provide new finishes, introduce new amenities, improve access or circulation to the building, add square footage, etc.

Sunrise
CAPITAL INVESTORS

LISTEN TO OUR PODCAST!

Real Estate Investing for

CASH
FLOW
with *Kevin Bupp*

★ ★ ★ ★ ★

WE HAVE LISTENERS IN OVER 190 COUNTRIES

Our popular podcasts teach listeners how to successfully invest in commercial real estate to generate cash flow and build legacy wealth

KevinBupp.com/podcast

DOWNLOAD

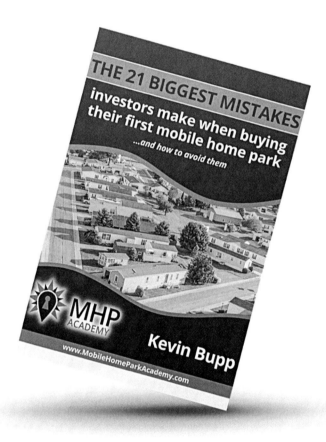

KevinBupp.com/MHPAcademy

INVEST ALONGSIDE
KEVIN BUPP
AND HIS TEAM AT

Sunrise
CAPITAL INVESTORS

Let's Grow Together

Real Estate Investing for
Cash Flow & Legacy Wealth

KevinBupp.com/Invest

DOWNLOAD THE INVESTOR'S

RESOURCE BUNDLE

- The Passive Investor's Guide to Mobile Home Park Investing
- The 21 Biggest Mistakes New MHP Investors Make
- Mobile Home Park Deal Analyzer
- Passive Investor's Guide to Parking Lot Profits
- Cold Call Script
- Letter of Intent (LOI) template

KevinBupp.com/FreeBundle

BRING KEVIN
A DEAL

Earn a $50k-$200k Finder's Fee
for any off-market deal you bring
that I close!

KevinBupp.com/Deal